C000229390

EAST
YORKSHIRE
CURIOSITIES

ROBERT WOODHOUSE

The History Press

First published 2010

The History Press
The Mill, Brimscombe Port
Stroud, Gloucestershire, GL5 2QG
www.thehistorypress.co.uk

© Robert Woodhouse, 2010

The right of Robert Woodhouse to be identified as the Author
of this work has been asserted in accordance with the
Copyrights, Designs and Patents Act 1988.

All rights reserved. No part of this book may be reprinted
or reproduced or utilised in any form or by any electronic,
mechanical or other means, now known or hereafter invented,
including photocopying and recording, or in any information
storage or retrieval system, without the permission in writing
from the Publishers.
British Library Cataloguing in Publication Data.
A catalogue record for this book is available from the British Library.

ISBN 978 0 7524 5619 5

Typesetting and origination by The History Press
Printed in Great Britain

Contents

ACKNOWLEDGEMENTS

Researching and composing material from such a wide geographical area has inevitably involved a considerable amount of travel and research. A great deal of assistance was provided both before and during visits by tourist information centres at Bridlington, Filey, York, Beverley and Kingston-upon-Hull.

Apart from the author's own collection of books, articles and press cuttings, information was gathered from local studies departments at several libraries including York, Beverley and Bridlington. Similar assistance with written material from their personal collections has been provided by Brian Sellers, Tony Barker and Arthur Flack.

Even with map references, some locations remained difficult to discover and it was on such occasions that traditional Yorkshire warmth and cooperation was in evidence. This was particularly the case at Wold Newton, Hunmanby, Kilham, Market Weighton and Flamborough. Thanks are also due to Sandra Mylan for typing and administrative services.

Few projects of this nature can be satisfactorily completed alone and again I owe a huge debt of gratitude to my wife, Sally, who has called on boundless measures of patience and enthusiasm in fulfilling a number of roles ranging from driver, navigator and map-reader to research assistant and proof reader.

INTRODUCTION

The area covered by this book corresponds roughly with the former East Riding of Yorkshire. The City of York has been included because, prior to becoming a non-metropolitan district in the county of North Yorkshire in 1974, York was a county borough with stronger links to settlements such as Hull, Bridlington and Beverley than other parts of Yorkshire.

Whereas the northern and western areas of Yorkshire are dominated by the high ground of moors and dales, the Wolds, along the eastern flank, do not possess the same grandeur. Yet centuries of human habitation have left intriguing features at locations such as Wold Newton, Kilham, Rudston and Goodmanham, along with the amazing stories that have unfolded at Wharram Percy.

The coastline of East Yorkshire and the Humber estuary offers several beguiling settings ranging from Filey Brigg to Flamborough Head and Spurn Point; but it is the man-made feature, 'Woodhenge', that dominates the countryside around Barmston, as does the Greek Temple of the Winds at Carnaby.

Threading across the East Yorkshire landscape, the Gypsey Race follows a tantalising course along clear channels before disappearing underground for stretches at a time, while it is often smaller, man-made structures – such as the lock-up at Workhouse Farm, Holme-upon-Spalding Moor – that provoke debate.

Church buildings invariably hold a range of compelling features. In the East Yorkshire area these include the memorial to a 'Boy Bishop' in St Oswald's Church at Filey; the medieval rood loft in Flamborough church; and the largest of all English parish churches, by area, namely Holy Trinity Church at Kingston-upon-Hull.

Continuous human occupation over a long period in the City of York has ensured a remarkable collection of curiosities. Many locations, such as the Shambles and All Hallows' Church in Goodramgate, attract countless visitors, but other settings are much less well known. From the captivating interior of The Blue Bell Inn in Fossgate, to the horned devil in Stonegate and the unusual layout of the Unitarian chapel in St Saviourgate, York has many aspects that will captivate and intrigue.

Robert Woodhouse, 2010

VISITING THE CURIOSITIES

The curiosities covered in this book are to be found in a wide range of locations. Several are landmarks and these are probably best viewed from a distance (especially when close inspection may involve a demanding ascent). At the same time, consideration should be given to wearing appropriate footwear, as ground conditions may well be soft or unstable.

A number of the properties are privately owned (as domestic or business premises) and must be viewed from the roadside, while others are subject to normal opening times (and may involve an admission charge). During the summer months several of the properties are opened on a limited basis and details are usually available from local tourist information centres.

The curiosities can be visited either singly or in groups. A few are in fairly remote countryside and can only be reached on foot, but the large majority are accessible by public transport. Special care should be taken along coastal stretches where cliff tops may well be unstable. Caution is also needed at locations beside lakes and waterways.

one

Filey and Bridlington

HUNMANBY LOCK-UP AND POUND

PLACES OF CUSTODY FOR WAYWARD LOCAL FOLK AND THEIR LIVESTOCK

Access

Lock-up and pinfold are on Hunmanby village green in the centre of the village.

Down the years many features of the traditional village green have disappeared, but at Hunmanby there are a couple of intriguing reminders of the days when village life seemed so much simpler than today.

For centuries the maintenance of law and order was in the hands of a parish constable, who was elected annually along with the churchwarden, the surveyor of the highways and the overseer of the poor. One of the constable's duties was to look after the village stocks; the use of stocks continued in some places until the mid-nineteenth century.

It was only by the second half of the nineteenth century, following the County and Borough Police Act of 1856, that the village bobby became a familiar figure and by this time small-scale lock-ups were in use as a means of detaining local wrongdoers.

Hunmanby's lock-up dates from 1834 and was said to become busier after disorderly scenes at annual local gatherings such as May Day celebrations, harvest events, the annual fair and Martinmas. Brick-built and oblong in shape, it is made up of twin cells and has a tablet inscribed with the date '1834'.

Close to the lock-up is the village pinfold where straying animals could be penned or impounded until their owners reclaimed them, usually after payment of a small fee to the pinder. This curious open-topped structure has been built with cobbles gathered from the nearby foreshore.

Hunmanby lock-up.

Hunmanby lock-up date stone.

Ancient Building

This Building is the Old Village Lock-Up erected in 1834. It was in frequent use after the annual fair & Martinmas which often ended in disorderly scenes. The Pinfold, built of Cobbles from the shore, was used to impound straying cattle.

Hunmanby lock-up information plaque.

Hunmanby pound.

HUNMANBY HALL LODGE

A MOCK MONASTIC RUIN

Access

Hunmanby
Hall gatehouse
and lodge is
adjacent to the
public road on
the west side
of the village.

During the late nineteenth century, the sporting Osbaldeston brothers held sway in this area of East Yorkshire. George was based a few miles away at Hutton Buscel and Humphrey Osbaldeston lived in Hunmanby Hall.

The main building dates from the late seventeenth century, but in 1809 Humphrey decided to construct an 'Early English' gateway. In spite of local opposition, Squire Osbaldeston used stones quarried from the coastal headland of Filey Brigg to complete a gatehouse in the style of a monastic ruin with small pointed windows on either side of a tall central arch.

Hunmanby arch.

ALL SAINTS' CHURCH, WOLD NEWTON

THE HUMBLEST OF BUILDINGS WITH OUTSTANDING NORMAN ARCHITECTURE

This simple place of worship, topped by a bell turret of timber and stone, provides a marked contrast to many other local churches which have been lavishly restored by the Sykes family of Sledmere.

Although the chancel and north aisle were rebuilt in the latter half of the nineteenth century, there are several striking features from the Norman period. A doorway on the south side has distinctive decorative symbols on the round arch and supporting capitals, while the tympanum displays a chequer pattern. The doorway has remained largely unrestored since it was first installed in the mid-twelfth century.

The interior includes a massive Norman chancel arch and a Norman window, along with medieval ones in the south wall of the nave, while the dainty drum-shaped Norman font completes this collection of fascinating features.

Access

All Saints' Church is located along the sloping hillside to the north of Wold Newton.

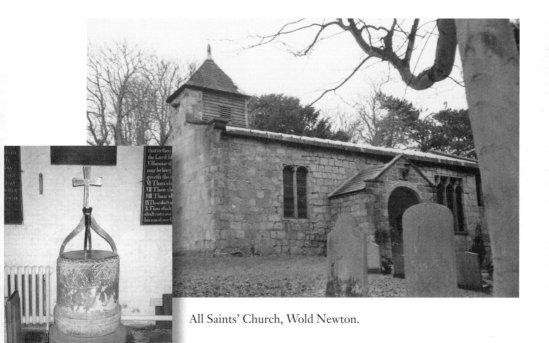

All Saints' Church, Wold Newton.

Font at All Saints' Church, Wold Newton.

LANGTOFT

UNHEAVENLY VISITATIONS FROM THE SKY

Access

Langtoft is approximately 6 miles north of Driffield on the B1249. Back Street is close to the centre of the village beside the Ship Inn on Scarborough Road

Freak weather conditions can strike any village or township almost without warning, but some locations seem to have suffered an unfair number of disasters in the face of raging elements.

In May 1853, two ploughmen working on farmland close to the village of Langtoft narrowly escaped death during a fierce thunderstorm. A bolt of lightening destroyed their ploughs and killed the attendant shire horses.

In June 1888 it was a different meteorological phenomenon that brought fear to the neighbourhood, when a waterspout swept mud and boulders from nearby hills through this quiet village setting. Any number of household items were gathered up and carried by the surging waters into the swollen village pond.

A commemorative plaque on the wall of a property in Back Street records the 'Great Floods' of 1657 and 1892. The height of the waters in 1657 is unknown but there are more details of the deluge that battered the village in 1892. Reaching a depth of 7½ft, the torrent swept off high ground into low-lying properties on Back Street, where household furniture, and items from a joiner's shop, were lifted from roadside properties and deposited some distance away.

A sign in Back Street, Langtoft.

Langtoft. Scene of a flood 3 July 1892.

GYPSEY STREAMS

WAYWARD, WHIMSICAL WATERCOURSES

In earlier days the gypsey streams of East Yorkshire attracted folklore and superstition; although many of these myths have now disappeared, these intriguing watercourses still hold a good deal of mystery.

The underlying chalk formation, with its network of underground reservoirs and natural conduits, explains the intermittent appearance and inexplicable disappearance of the gypseys (the name is probably derived from the Norse word *gypa*, which means 'to gush').

By the seventeenth century, the appearance of these gypsey springs had become associated with dramatic events such as the Great Plague of London in 1665-6. A greater torrent, known as the Woe Waters, was said to have preceded events of national importance such as the restoration of the monarchy, the landing of William of Orange and the two world wars. At a local level this natural phenomenon was linked with serious storms and the fall of the meteorite at Wold Newton in 1795.

The Gypsey Race (the best-known of the streams) runs for approximately 22 miles across the wide floor of the Great Wold Valley. Beginning at Wharram, it usually flows above ground to Wold Newton, where it disappears underground before emerging again to the north-west of Rudston. A spring that rises near the famous monolith soon joins the Gypsey Race, which now veers eastwards to curve through the grounds of Thorpe Hall. After another 2 miles it runs across land surrounding Boynton Hall before reaching the North Sea at Bridlington Quay.

One strange characteristic of the Gypsey Race is that it often begins to flow after a dry season, and at times a whole host of additional springs appear like silver threads in the centre of ploughed fields and open pastures alongside the main channel. Folklore refers to these as the awe-inspiring aforementioned Woe Waters.

In recent times, drainage operations and water extraction schemes have affected the course and intensity of the Gypsey Race, but this whimsical watercourse is still to be found pursuing an often intermittent and unpredictable route from Wharram to the sea at Bridlington.

Access

The Gypsey Race may be seen at Ruston (4½ miles from Bridlington on B1253) or at Boynton (3 miles from Bridlington) or at Wold Newton (10 miles from Bridlington via Burton Fleming)

Gypsey Race at Wold Newton.

KILHAM

FROM BULL BAITING TO THE PIGEON CORPS

Access

Kilham is about 8 miles west of Bridlington via A614 (Bridlington to Driffield road).

Quieter times have returned to Kilham in recent years but there are still several intriguing reminders of the village's heyday as 'Capital of the Wolds'. Neighbouring slopes have provided burials, ornaments and a range of artefacts that indicate continuous settlement from the Bronze Age, and the walls of All Saints' Church, at the heart of the village, has many fragments of Norman carved stones as well as a splendid Norman doorway of five orders of zig-zag decoration.

A plaque in the churchyard gives details of the village's importance as a market centre and an iron ring set in a block of stone serves as a reminder of the time when the baiting of animals was regarded as entertainment. (Such so-called sports were declared illegal by Act of Parliament in 1849.)

Close to the war memorial, in the churchyard, a sundial is set on top of a strange weathered stone that resembles a small empty coffin.

All Saints' Church, Kilham.

During the Second World War, Kilham was the base for the Pigeon Corps, which played a crucial, if rather obscure, role in communications. Secret messages were carried by pigeons when secrecy was a major consideration or when other methods of communication had failed.

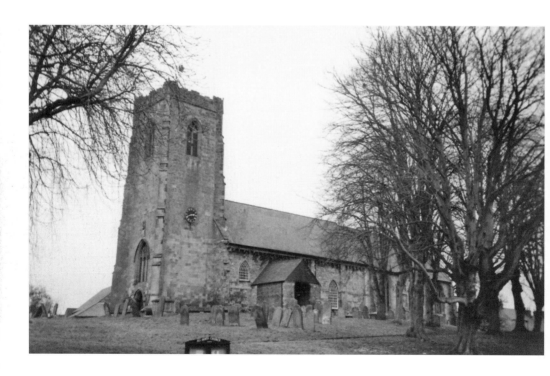

An information plaque in Kilham churchyard.

Bull ring at Kilham.

Sundial in Kilham churchyard.

Kilham village.

RUDSTON MONOLITH

DEVIL'S JAVELIN OR PLACE OF WORSHIP

Access

Rudston is 4½ miles from Bridlington via the B1253 and All Saints' Church is located on high ground on the south side of the village.

The pretty village of Rudston is the unlikely setting for Britain's tallest standing stone. Measuring some 25ft 9in in height, and with two large flat faces spreading about 5ft from edge to edge, this amazing mass dominates the north-east side of All Saints' churchyard.

The top of the stone has been weathered away over the years and is now covered by a protective metal cap, so it could in fact have been taller. Estimates of the weight of the massive monolith suggest between 30 and 40 tonnes.

Local folklore states that the Devil was so enraged by the building of a church on his revered summit that he slung a stone javelin at it. Narrowly missing the intended target, it was embedded in its present position.

Close examination of the stone surfaces reveals possible fossilised dinosaur footprints on one side; this could have heightened its importance for our early ancestors. This huge lump of grit stone is thought to have been quarried and hauled from Cayton Bay some 10 miles away on the south side of Scarborough,

and experts date its installation at Rudston to about 2000 BC. There is plenty of speculation about methods of transporting such a large stone; it is thought that a significant part of the journey could have been made by water along the River Derwent or River Rye and then across the Vale of Pickering, which would still have been covered, in part, by a deep-water lake. Following its transfer from raft to sledge, the final stages of the journey could have seen the stone dragged over a long line of rounded logs to its destination at Rudston.

Suggestions regarding its use include its possible installation as a tribute to a Sun God or as an act of thanksgiving for the spring that flows from a nearby hill – but the consensus seems to be that it was used for religious ceremonies and rituals.

All Saints' Church and monolith, Rudston.

BOYNTON CHURCH

UNUSUAL REMINDERS OF THE STRICKLAND FAMILY

St Andrew's Church at Boynton stands alongside the lane leading to Boynton Hall. Although the exterior is uninspiring, there are many fascinating aspects within the sturdy walls.

The altar, pews and woodwork are painted in a subtle matt green colour to provide a gentle backdrop for features such as the columns which support a gallery at the west end, and the chancel arch. Initial impressions seem to indicate classical architectural designs, but closer inspection reveals an unusual Egyptian influence.

At a lower level, the lectern is topped not by the customary eagle but by a turkey which became the crest of the Strickland family. Based at nearby Boynton Hall, several members of the Strickland household distinguished themselves in different walks of life.

Access

Boynton church and hall are about 4 miles north-east of Bridlington via the A165 and B1253.

St Andrew's Church, Boynton.

Font in St Andrew's Church, Boynton.   Turkey lectern in St Andrew's Church, Boynton.

Walter Strickland and Sir William Strickland played important roles in the turbulent times of the English Civil War and Restoration of the Monarchy under Charles II. Sir George Strickland wrote an important review of agricultural practices and published a valuable map of Yorkshire, while Sir Charles Strickland is said to have been the original Martin in *Tom Brown's Schooldays*. But it is the first William Strickland of Boynton that is linked with the family's heraldic symbol.

As a young man, William Strickland left his quiet East Yorkshire home to sail from Bristol to the New World on a voyage of discovery and exploration with Sebastian Cabot. This celebrated Italian navigator is commonly credited with the discovery of the turkey and it would appear that the youthful member of the Strickland household was 'turkey boy' on the expedition, with responsibility for the birds on the voyage and overall supervision when they reached England.

William Strickland accumulated considerable wealth from the profits of his voyages and applied for a coat-of-arms incorporating a simple picture of the turkey. The original picture of his crest, 'a turkey in his pride', was lodged at the College of Arms and is widely regarded as the first known picture of a turkey.

BAPTIST CHAPEL IN OLD BRIDLINGTON

ONE OF THE SMALLEST AND EARLIEST NON-CONFORMIST PLACES OF WORSHIP

Long before Bridlington's heyday as a popular holiday resort, the original township flourished round the walls of the priory buildings. Bridlington Priory was established for the Augustinian Canons between AD 1115 and 1120 by Walter de Gant, but the earliest surviving stonework dates from the early thirteenth century.

Applegarth Lane, close to the Bayle, or gatehouse, was originally the orchard of the priory and here, in 1699, a simple chapel was constructed by a Scottish farmer whose ship had been driven by a gale into Bridlington Bay.

Measuring only 12ft square and with only twenty founder members, it represents the first Baptist chapel to be established in East Yorkshire. In its present state, neglected and unused, it represents a tangible, although forlorn, reminder of this area's varied religious history.

Access

Bridlington is 16 miles south of Scarborough on the A165. Applegarth Lane is on the south side of the Bayle Museum in Kirkgate.

Old Bridlington former Baptist chapel.

HARPHAM

ST JOHN'S CHURCH AND LEGENDARY WELLS

Access

Harpham
is about 8
miles west of
Bridlington
via the A166.
The wells are
located in open
ground beyond
St John's
Church.

The Church of St John of Beverley at Harpham contains several links with the St Quintin family, who held land in these parts from the medieval period until the nineteenth century. A field on the south side of the church once marked the site of an early home of the St Quintins, but all that remains today is the so-called Drummer's Well.

Legends suggest that the lord of the manor and fellow nobles were staging a tournament of field sports in the fourteenth century when St Quintin accidentally knocked his drummer boy, Tom Hewson, into the well. Rescue attempts proved fruitless and the young lad drowned with the result that his mother, the village soothsayer, prophesied that a sound of drumming from the well would herald the death of a member of the St Quintin family.

Another well at the east end of the village is said to be named after St John of Beverley, who was born in AD 640. (It is claimed that he was born in the village, although Cherry Burton also lays claim to being his birthplace.) One legend associated with the well is that a defeated army arrived in the village, whereupon St John drove his staff into the ground causing an endless flow of pure drinking water.

St John's tomb in Beverley Minster is decorated each springtime with primroses collected from local woods by the young people of Harpham. On the nearest Tuesday to St John's Day (7 May) choirboys from Beverley Minster traditionally filed from Harpham church to the decorated well.

St John's Well, Harpham.

Drummer's Well, Harpham.

ST OSWALD'S CHURCH, FLAMBOROUGH

MAGNIFICENT MEDIEVAL ROOD LOFT

St Oswald's Church saw some rebuilding during the nineteenth century but retains a Norman font and chancel arch with rich moulding and tilting sides. Much of the detail on the arch is hidden by a magnificent medieval screen which spans the width of the church.

'Rood' is the old term for a cross or crucifix – usually the great crucifix set on the screen which divided the nave and chancel – and many churches had a gallery or rood loft extending along the top from which parts of the service were conducted.

Many of these rood lofts were destroyed during the Reformation and only two survive in Yorkshire (the other one being at Hubberholme in Wharfedale).

St Oswald's screen dates from the fifteenth century and has a row of solid panels enriched with a series of thirteen canopies of delicate tabernacle work. Above the canopies are graceful bands of vine carving and quatrefoils, while the lower level has an attractive strip of trailing roses and leaves. This superb piece of craftsmanship still shows traces of gold and other coloured paintwork and it is believed that it was first installed at nearby Bridlington Priory.

Access

Flamborough village is about 4 miles east of Bridlington via the B1255.

Rood loft in St Oswald's Church, Flamborough.

FLAMBOROUGH

FASCINATING LINKS WITH THE CONSTABLE FAMILY

Access

The remains of Flamborough Castle are in the centre of a field on the north side of St Oswald's Church.

A ruined section of walled building surrounded by grassy mounds in the centr of a large field offers a clue to the powerful dynasty that once held sway along this section of Yorkshire's coastline. The crumbling masonry was part of fortified manor house belonging to the Constable family, but apart from trace of a vaulted ceiling there are no other indications of their controlling influence.

The Constables were based at Flamborough from the thirteenth century and one curious tale suggests that by the early 1500s the family were unsure abou who should receive their payments of rent. According to legend, Sir Marmaduke Constable believed it was due to the King of Denmark and each year he made his way to the cliff top and fired an arrow, with a gold coin attached, far out to sea. As the arrow soared skywards he called out that if anyone chose to come fo it, he was ready to pay his rent to the King of Denmark.

Flamborough Castle.

Sir Marmaduke and his son, Robert, fought the Scots at Flodden Field in 1513, and Robert was later knighted at Blackheath for his bravery in the Cornish Rising. His fortunes changed during the 1530s when he joined the Pilgrimage of Grace, a revolt by northern barons against the closure of monasteries by Henry VIII, for he was found guilty of treason and put to death at Hull.

During the seventeenth century, Sir William Constable narrowly escaped execution for treason and was then imprisoned by Charles I for holding out against the Ship Tax. He fought for Parliament at Edgehill, took command of the siege of Scarborough and played a leading role in the decisive Battle of Marston Moor before signing the death warrant of the king. Sir William was buried in Westminster Abbey, but on the Restoration of the Monarchy under Charles II, in 1660, his body was removed along with the mortal remains of Cromwell and Blake.

The tomb of Sir Marmaduke Constable is in the chancel of St Oswald's Church in Flamborough. A brass on the tomb has a curious rhyming epitaph, which explains that he was a man of great bravery who fought in France for Edward IV's army and played a major role at Flodden Field at the age of seventy. He lived through six reigns and his death in 1518 is linked with a strange tale of a toad eating his heart. This gruesome account is illustrated on the tomb, where the sculptor has depicted the breast of a man exposed to show the heart.

Memorial to Sir
Marmaduke Constable,
St Oswald's Church,
Flamborough.

FLAMBOROUGH'S LIGHTHOUSES

FLASHING A WARNING TO SEA-GOING MEN

Access

Flamborough
Head and
the two
lighthouses
are about 2
miles east of
Flamborough
village via the
B1259.

With the advent of global positioning equipment, lighthouses might appear to have become redundant – but this is far from the case, as several of these Yorkshire coastal sentinels still flash their messages into the darkness.

Two lighthouses are still in position at Spurn Point, though neither is operational; nor is the landmark tower in Withernsea centre, but it is a different story at Flamborough, Whitby and Scarborough. Scarborough lighthouse has given its name to the location where it is based, known as Lighthouse Pier, although its correct name is St Vincent's Pier. Whitby lighthouse is positioned to the east of the town and there are smaller lights on the harbour's east and west piers.

Best known of Yorkshire's lighthouses, and the only one open to the public, is at Flamborough Head. Completed in 1806, to designs by Samuel Wyatt, construction work took only five months at a total cost of £8,000 for the 92 ft-high tower and linked keeper's house. The loss of 174 ships in the previous thirty-six

Flamborough lighthouse.

Flamborough's old lighthouse, built in 1674.

years had convinced Trinity House, the maritime corporation established in 1514 for supervision of all lighthouses and beacons, of the need for a reliable, durable lighthouse on Flamborough Head. It was the first British lighthouse to display two white flashes followed by red from a set of oil-burning lamps. During foggy episodes it also fired rockets 600ft into the sky to give further warning of the treacherous coastline.

In more recent times, four white flashes are transmitted every fifteen seconds with a range of 24 miles visibility out in the North Sea. Until 1996 keepers were still based at Flamborough, but today's operations are entirely automatic and controlled from a Trinity House depot in Harwich.

An earlier lighthouse stands close to the public road leading to Flamborough Head. Regarded as the oldest surviving lighthouse in England, the 79ft-high chalk tower was built by Sir John Clayton in 1674. The warning beacon consisted of a coal fire in an iron basket on top of the octagonal tower. Sir John planned to fund operations by tolls charged on passing ships. The scheme inevitably proved to be impractical and restoration work has suggested that this early lighthouse was hardly used.

FLAMBOROUGH HEAD

MAJESTIC SETTING FOR NATURAL BEAUTY AND HUMAN DRAMA

Access

Cliff-top paths from Bridlington and Flamborough offer seaward views and access to Thornwick Bay and North and South Landing.

The dramatic cliff tops of Flamborough Head must rank as one of the fines viewpoints along the whole of England's eastern coastline. A wall of glistening chalk rises around 170ft above North Sea breakers, taking in Speeton, Buckton and Bempton Cliffs before reaching a dramatic conclusion on the promontory of Flamborough Head.

This magnificent natural spectacle is famous for its seabirds, with ledges offering shelter for countless families of razorbills, guillemots, kittiwakes and puffins, while the relentless battering from the North Sea has fashioned amazing rock formations and mysterious caves. Three of the caves are known as S George's Hole, Smuggler's Cave and Robin Lythe's Hole. The latter, a cavernous hollow with a 50ft-high roof, has associations with a smuggler named Robin Lythe, whose escapades are recalled in R.D. Blackmore's novel *Mary Anerley*.

Flamborough Head.

A series of tiny coves, including Thornwick Bay, South Landing and North Landing, have witnessed many dramatic shipwrecks and epic rescue attempts, as well as any number of human dramas.

In 1406, a youthful Prince James of Scotland was captured by English forces - either at sea, off the headland, or in the nearby village – and taken under guard to Windsor, where he was held prisoner for nineteen years. During this period of imprisonment James built a reputation as a scholar and poet, and met and married Lady Joan Somerset who travelled back to Scotland with him as his queen.

On the evening of 23 September 1779, Flamborough Head became the viewpoint for a dramatic naval battle between a fleet of four American warships and two British man-of-war ships that were escorting a large group of merchant vessels returning from the Baltic region.

The American naval commander was John Paul Jones and his boat, *Bonhomme Richard*, was soon engaged in a fierce engagement with Richard Pearson's *Serapis*. Already outgunned, Jones soon lost two of his biggest guns in an explosion, causing him to opt for close-quarter fighting. With the two ships lashed together, the tide of battle was turning against Jones until a grenade thrown by one of his crew caused dozens of casualties on the British vessel.

Although the *Bonhomme Richard* sank, John Paul Jones triumphed against superior British forces and sailed the *Serapis* to Texel in Holland before being fêted by Louis XVI in France. His exploits assumed legendary proportions and John Paul Jones is often referred to as the 'Father of the American Navy'.

During the last thirty years there have been several systematic surveys of the seabed of Bridlington Bay, but so far all efforts to locate and recover evidence from the *Bonhomme Richard* have proved unsuccessful.

Stack off Flamborough Head.

BRIDLINGTON PRIORY AND THE BAYLE

RIDDLE IN STONE FROM THE HEYDAY OF MONASTERIES

Access

The Bayle and Bridlington Priory are on the east side of Scarborough Road.

The Bayle, or gatehouse, is an unlikely neighbour for Bridlington Priory, yet it represents the only monastic building to survive intact after the Dissolution of the Monasteries. Dating from about 1390, the Bayle Gate is in a fine state of preservation (with restoration work visible at the upper level, completed in the seventeenth and eighteenth centuries).

Beyond a spreading archway, a vaulted roof has stone corbels decorated with a king, a monk and bagpipes. From this ground-floor level, a stairway leads to an upper room, measuring about 60ft in length and 30ft wide. Down the centuries this fascinating room has housed the prior's court and served as a prison, Non-conformist meeting room and school, before its current use as a museum.

Following closure of the priory by Henry VIII's commissioners, most of the buildings on the site were demolished and sections of the church, including the choir, transepts and central tower, have also disappeared. Remaining parts, such as the nave, north porch and two west towers, form an impressive fragment of the overall structure. The west front is particularly powerful and unusual.

Side by side, and in dazzling contrast, we can make out the simple, controlled lines of the thirteenth and fourteenth-century north-west tower and the extravagant fifteenth-century decoration in the south-west tower and gabled end of the nave. (Both towers above clerestory level date from the 1870s, when Sir G. Gilbert Scott carried out restoration work.)

The Bayle, Old Bridlington.

WILLIAM KENT

LINK WITH ONE OF THIS COUNTRY'S FOREMOST LANDSCAPE DESIGNERS

A simple plaque on a High Street property in Old Bridlington serves as a reminder that one of this country's early designers spent his formative years in the township.

Born in 1785, William Kent grew up in this busy Georgian setting before heading to the continent in 1710 to further his study of painting. During his stay in Rome, Kent met young men such as Lord Burlington (1716) and Thomas Coke (1714 and 1718) who were making the Grand Tour of art galleries, museums and classical sites.

On his return to England in 1719, William Kent became the leading figure in a group of artists associated with Lord Burlington. Initially he worked as an artist and decorated the interior of many eighteenth-century houses, but he also turned his hand to designing furniture and then moved into the field of architecture – most notably at Holkham Hall.

Much of his later work involved designing smaller buildings and landscapes in places such as Claremont, Chiswick, Stowe and Rousham in Oxfordshire. Kent's characteristic achievement was said to be an ability to soften landscape features in order to open up distant panoramas. Inspiration for his ideas allegedly came from Italian paintings and landscapes, as well as Chinese influences, but maybe some of his designs featuring meandering paths, winding rivers and scattered trees originated from those childhood years in East Yorkshire.

Access

The High Street in Old Bridlington is just to the south of the A165 Scarborough Road.

Plaque relating to William Kent, High Street, Old Bridlington.

FILEY'S CHURCH BRIDGE

RE-WORKED WROUGHT IRONWORK SPANNING THE RAVINE

Access

Church Bridge
spans Church
Ravine at the
northern end
of Filey where
it links Church
Street with
St Oswald's
Church.

Recycled ironwork from North Yorkshire railway routes has found an unlikely setting on Filey's Church Bridge, where it provides access from Church Street to St Oswald's Church.

Stark brick walls on either side of Church Ravine form a contrast with the decorative ironwork and converted gas lamps of the central span, while an information panel gives details of the bridge's improbable ironwork.

Church
Bridge,
Filey.

Information
plaque,
Church
Bridge,
Filey.

SPRING WATER

A NATURAL SUPPLY OF ADAM'S ALE

Natural greenery now covers the troughs that held drinking water for local people before the advent of mains water supplies. Set on the southern side of Church Ravine, this spring provided fresh water for locals for hundreds of years. It was also used by visiting Dutch fishing fleets, who rolled barrels up the slope from the beach to collect valuable quantities of Adam's ale.

Access

The well is set on the southern slope of Church Ravine at the northern end of Filey.

Well in Church Ravine, Filey.

A 'BOY BISHOP'

HIGH OFFICE FOR THE CHOSEN YOUTH

Access

St Oswald's
Church is on
the north side
of Church
Ravine via
A1039
Scarborough
Road.

St Oswald's Church at Filey is dedicated to the patron saint of fishermen and a impressive memorial window, installed in 1885 and regarded as the Fishermen Window, recalls local men lost at sea.

Close by, on the wall of the south aisle, is a carved stone figure with a larg nose and long-sleeved gown. His head is resting on cushions and this 'Bo Bishop' is said to be linked with a strange ceremony that dates back more tha 700 years.

It was probably carved between 1250 and 1300 and may well have been i tribute to a 'Boy Bishop' who died in office. A 'Boy Bishop' was elected in larg parishes, from the choir or grammar school, to serve as the leading character i a range of Church festivals during the Midd Ages.

From 6 December, St Nicholas' Day, throug to Holy Innocents' Day on 28 December, th elected youth was endowed with the fu insignia of a bishop, with responsibility fo conducting church services and supervisin the behaviour of boys dressed as priest This strange arrangement came to be see as blasphemous and irreverent after th Reformation and was abolished.

Another more gruesome theory is that th figure represents a 'heart burial' of one of th Augustinian Canons from nearby Bridlingto Priory. During the medieval period, it wa common for a wealthy individual to have h heart buried in a favoured church below miniature carving of himself.

Originally this intriguing stone featur would have been laid horizontally. It narrowl escaped destruction during restoratio work in 1893, when John Fox prevailed on workman not to crush it. He is said to hav rewarded the labourer with a pint of local al

'Boy Bishop' in St Oswald's Church, Filey.

ST OSWALD'S CHURCH, FILEY

IN SEARCH OF FASCINATING EXTERNAL FEATURES

The earliest phase of building work at St Oswald's Church took place between 1180 and 1230, with additions and alterations made during the late thirteenth, fourteenth and fifteenth centuries. Many of its ancient features were destroyed at the time of restoration work in 1839 but internally the church presents a pleasing blend of building styles and sensitive modernisation schemes. Externally, St Oswald's has powerfully direct outlines dominated by the crossing tower and a closer inspection of the exterior reveals a number of interesting features.

A buttress on the south-east corner of the chancel shows the extent of the wall's tilt towards the ravine, while a tiny window at the west end of the church was meant to admit light to a staircase leading into the western tower. The tower, however, was never constructed.

Access

St Oswald's Church is on the north side of Church Ravine via A1039 Scarborough Road.

St Oswald's Church, Filey.

Mason's mark, St Oswald's Church, Filey.

Close to the priest's door, on the south wall of the chancel, is a 'Mass Clock', which has an inscribed dial to denote times for celebration of Mass. Above the vestry door, on the north-west corner, is a mason's mark, showing a ladder to illustrate the Old Testament story of Jacob's dream.

Set on top of the tower is a weathervane in the shape of a fish, which probably represents the early settlement's links with the fishing industry.

ROMAN STONES

CLUES FROM THE FINAL DAYS OF THE ROMAN OCCUPATION OF BRITAIN

Access

The Roman Stones are in Crescent Gardens between The Crescent and the cliff top overlooking Filey Sands.

Set among heathers and decorative pebbles in gardens beside The Crescent, a group of five square stones may hardly warrant a second glance. Yet a closer look at an information panel reveals a fascinating aspect of Filey's early history.

The 'Roman Stones' were uncovered when a landslip at Carr Naze, at the northern end of Filey Sands, exposed a section of wall together with charred wood, bones and pottery. Initial inspection of this shoreline site was carried out by a painter named Wilson; Revd Richard Brooke organised further examination. He found walls made of large stones, set in mortar and extending 4ft below ground to a bed of puddle clay, which enclosed a large stone floor. In the centre were five large stones, which were at first thought to be Roman altars but were later determined to be bases for pillars – probably part of a wooden structure. In the top of each stone was a socket measuring 7in square and 3in deep, and the nearby presence of charred timbers gave an indication of the fate of this tower.

The tall central wooden structure was part of a Roman signal station and represents the most southerly of a series of such look-out positions extending from Huntcliff, near Saltburn, that were built towards the end of the Roman occupation of this country (late fourth century). The threat to Roman troops and civilians came from North European tribes and Pictish tribes from northern areas of mainland Britain.

Roman Stones, Filey.

A base for a pillar,
Roman Stones, Filey.

FILEY BRIGG

AN ARRAY OF NATURAL AND MAN-MADE PHENOMENA

Access

Filey Brigg can
be reached
via the A1039
Scarborough
Road on the
north side of
Filey, where
Church Ravine
and Cliff Drive
reach the
country park
leading to the
Brigg.

Local folklore suggests that Filey Brigg (a rock promontory) resulted from the Devil's plan to construct a causeway from the Yorkshire coast across the North Sea. When he abandoned the scheme, the Prince of Darkness is said to have dropped his hammer into the ocean, and when he dipped his hand into the water to recover it, he clasped a fish between his thumb and finger. This accounts for the distinctive markings of the haddock.

In fact this impressive headland, measuring about ¾ mile in length, is an entirely natural outcrop that was formed by a geological fault. The name 'Brigg' is derived from a Scandinavian term for 'landing place' although, in reality, its rocky ridges represent a serious hazard to shipping. As well as the site of the Roman signal station, there is further evidence of human occupation in the form of a high earth rampart that dates from the Anglo Saxon or Viking period. But it is the geological formation, along with rich bird and plant life, that have led to Filey Brigg's designation as a Site of Special Scientific Interest.

An open grassy area at the landward side of the Brigg marks the eastern end of two National Trails – the Cleveland Way and Wolds Way – and for many years these open slopes offered a fine vantage point for viewing a couple of curious local customs.

Filey Bay was traditionally located within the manor of Hunmanby and lords of the manor displayed their authority by performing well-established ceremonies. During a ritual involving the 'dragnet', an empty net was hauled along the shoreline in order to demonstrate that the lords of the manor held salvage rights along the coast. Press reports from 1911 indicate that the net was dragged, by horsepower, for a distance of around 5 miles from Filey Brigg to towering cliffs on the north side of Flamborough Head.

The south
face of Filey
Brigg.

Another long-standing ceremony continued at Filey Bay until 1928 and involved the throwing of a javelin from the beach. The background to this strange ritual remains unclear, but it seems that the point where the tip of the javelin struck the seabed marked the limit for inshore fishing. After a lapse of many years the ceremony was re-established by Sir Dennis Readett Bayley (1878-1940) who leased Hunmanby Hall before taking over ownership of the estate and its associated traditions in 1919.

DANES' DYKE

A MAN-MADE BARRIER OF IMMENSE PROPORTIONS

There are several examples of early hill forts in rural areas of Yorkshire, including sites at Boltby Scar, Roulston Scar and Eston Nab where a defensive ditch has been cut through a natural promontory. The grandest location, though, is to be found on the North Sea coast at Flamborough.

Running directly north to south, and about a mile to the west of Flamborough village, this massive earthwork encloses an area of around 5 square miles of the Yorkshire coastline. Though the sides and bottom of the huge ditch are now covered in trees, its dimensions are still impressive. Banks rising 18ft in height line a west-facing ditch that measures 60ft across and there are traces of a second bank outside the ditch.

Its name, 'Danes' Dyke', is misleading, for it is generally accepted that this enormous man-made earthwork was constructed during the Iron Age period – probably the first century AD – at a time of inter-tribal warfare.

Access

The B1229 and B1255 roads running east from the A165 cut through Danes' Dyke on the way to Flamborough village.

Danes' Dyke.

CARNABY TEMPLE

AN EYE-CATCHING RURAL FOLLY

Set on high ground to the north-west of Carnaby village, this tall two-storey brick tower makes a dramatic landmark feature. It was built in 1770 for Sir William Strickland of Boynton Hall and is said to be based on the Temple of Winds in Athens.

Incorporating a lantern top section, the double curve of the roof (ogee style) features a trend that was popular in the fourteenth century.

This elevated setting in the Carnaby Temple made a fine look-out position and, during a long period of occupation, a low-level outbuilding was added at the rear. In recent years it has remained empty, but maintenance work on the fabric ensures that this splendid folly retains a considerable amount of grandeur.

Access

Carnaby Temple stands on open ground between the villages of Carnaby and Boynton, about 2½ miles from Bridlington.

Carnaby Temple.

SETTRINGTON HOUSE GATEWAY

UNUSUAL DESIGN WORK

Access

Settrington is
4½ miles from
Malton via the
B1248 road to
Driffield.

Settrington village is composed mainly of identical, stone-built estate cottages dating from the early part of the nineteenth century. Apart from All Saints' Church, the main building is Settrington House – which was completed during the 1790s, although a serious fire in 1963 resulted in reconstruction of the central block with single and double-storeyed sections.

It is the gateway leading to Settrington House that holds particular interest. Whereas most country houses boast solid stone gateways, handsomely decorated with coats-of-arms and imperious animals or birds, those at Settrington House are fashioned in wrought iron with the top sections showing a stork. Closer examination shows that these slim birds are carrying small bundles in their claws. These probably represent scallop shells, which traditionally symbolise pilgrims.

Settrington
House
gateway.

ST NICHOLAS' CHURCH, NORTH GRIMSTON

DRAMATIC CARVED FEATURES ON A MASSIVE NORMAN FONT

Much of St Nicholas' simple stonework dates from the thirteenth century, but the interior is dominated by a number of features from the Norman period. Apart from two highly unusual internal buttresses and a low, wide chancel arch, it is the extraordinary Norman font that catches the eye.

Measuring more than 3ft in diameter, this huge stone drum is covered on the outside with bold, clear carvings. More than half of the surface shows the Lord and his disciples at the Last Supper, with details of the meal including fish, bread and goblets all clearly portrayed on the table. The disciples are shown in faintly-patterned robes and many have a knife in one hand and a book in the other.

The rest of the font illustrates the Descent from the Cross, and is claimed to be the only font with this representation. In this instance it is a Maltese cross and one figure has his arms around the Lord; a nearby figure with a staff is thought to be St Nicholas.

Access

North Grimston is on the B1248 Malton to Beverley road, about 6 miles from Malton.

The font at St Nicholas' Church, North Grimston.

St Nicholas' Church, North Grimston.

ST ANDREW'S CHURCH, WEAVERTHORPE

UNUSUAL FEATURES IN CHURCH AND CHURCHYARD

Access

Weaverthorpe
is about 16
miles east of
Malton on
the A64 via
Sherburn.

The lofty, slender tower of St Andrew's Church is reminiscent of similar structures in Northumberland and with slim, narrow windows in both the tower and adjoining staircase turret, it has the appearance of a fortified border refuge.

Above the Norman doorway is a fine Saxon sundial with the Latin inscription: *'Herbertus Wintonie hoc monasterium fecit'* – Herbert of Winchester built this church. Inside there is a Norman tub font with a carved pattern decorating its surface.

It is generally agreed that restoration work, carried out in 1872 by G.E. Street for Sir Tatton Sykes of Sledmere, has enhanced the interior. His additions include splendid barrel roofs (made up of twenty-six ribs in the nave and fifteen ribs in the chancel), a brass chancel screen with a pattern of leaves and scrolls, and a pulpit fashioned from wrought iron on a stone base.

A squat column in St Andrew's churchyard.

St Andrew's Church, Weaverthorpe.

A curious squat column, made up of circular layers, beside the churchyard path is also linked with Sir Tatton Sykes. This puzzling structure was originally topped with a cross and, according to local knowledge, it served as a memorial to local people who were buried without a gravestone. (It seems that the cross was destroyed in gales during the 1980s.)

WOLD NEWTON METEORITE

AN UNEXPECTED MISSILE FROM OUTER SPACE

Meteorite landings are fairly uncommon, and it is highly unusual to have an eye-witness account of such a dramatic event. Yet this happened in the remote rural setting of Wold Newton, some 5 miles south-west of Filey, on Sunday afternoon, 13 December 1795, as shepherd John Shipley was making his way across open fields near Wold Cottage.

According to contemporary reports, a thunderstorm was raging across the Yorkshire Wolds when the clouds parted and a white-hot lump of stone hurtled through the sky to bury itself within yards of the terrified farm worker. Curiously, the meteorite crashed to earth at exactly 3 p.m. and other eyewitnesses, including an estate carpenter and a groom, were able to add details to the momentous event.

During the final seconds of its dramatic journey to earth – at a speed of about 50 metres per second – the meteorite narrowly missed Wold Cottage, home of Captain Edward Topham. He was in London at the time but immediately made his way back to Wold Newton in order to carry out a full investigation.

The stone was found to have passed through around 9in of topsoil before coming to rest in the underlying chalk formation. After it had been recovered, Captain Topham displayed the meteorite in London for viewing by 'the curious, and the public in general', with an admission charge of one shilling. He also financed construction of a brick obelisk to mark the site of the meteorite's landing. An inscription on the stone table records:

Here
On this spot, December 13, 1795
Fell from the atmosphere
An extraordinary stone
In breadth twenty eight inches
In length thirty six inches
And
Whose weight was fifty-six pounds
This column
In memory of it
Was erected by
Edward Topham
1799

The meteorite is now held in London's Natural History Museum, but there are several reminders of this momentous event in the Wolds area. Apart from the obelisk, which is on private land, the village inn at nearby Thwing was named

Access

Wold Newton is 16 miles east of Malton, between the villages of Thwing and Fordon.

after the meteorite, while ale produced at the Wold Top microbrewery has bee
named 'Falling Stone Bitter'.

Meteorite impacts are few and far between because most burn up as the
reach the upper atmosphere and provide displays of 'shooting stars' – but ther
is evidence of at least two other landings in North Yorkshire.

A meteorite fall at Pennyman's Sidings, near Ormesby village to the south c
Middlesbrough, on 14 March 1881, was witnessed by railway workers; and, a
recently as August 2005, another meteorite was excavated on the escarpment c
the Hambleton Hills near the village of Kilburn.

Wold Newton obelisk.

two

Driffield and Hornsea

BETTISON'S FOLLY, HORNSEA

AN IMPRESSIVE MEALTIME OBSERVATION

Access

Hornsea is midway between Bridlington and Hull and about 12 miles from Beverley via the A1035 and B1244.

Set among modern housing on Willows Drive, and almost engulfed by tall trees, Bettison's Folly soars around 50ft from ground level to a crenellated upper section. Dark brown misshapen bricks protrude from the circular walls of this look-out tower that was constructed, so it is reported, so that Mr Bettison could be sure of a piping-hot meal on his return home. Evidently servants were detailed to watch along the Hull Road for Mr Bettison's carriage so that a meal could be served as soon as he came through the door.

Bettison's Folly,
Hornsea.

The doorway of Bettison's Folly.

It is also claimed that Bettison's Folly is one of only two follies in the country with a retractable flagpole – the other one is Powderham Belvedere in Devon – and, according to tradition, the English flag is flown annually on St George's Day.

There is no sign of William Bettison's nearby residence but his tower still stands imperiously within its fringe of trees.

'WOODHENGE' AT BARMSTON

STRANGE SET OF SOARING TIMBERS

Access

From Chapel Lane in Barmston, a footpath runs beyond a stile and across the field to woodland where it continues to the right-hand corner of the field and across the end of the wood.

As the North Sea creeps ever closer to the straggling village of Barmston, a curious man-made creation stands defiantly on a nearby hilltop. With obvious similarities to the major monument on Salisbury Plain, it has become known as 'Woodhenge', though it is composed of single, slender tree trunks (rather than a trio of sections).

Dramatic and evocative, it was the work of a local landowner, Chris Marshall, and is believed to represent a memorial to death. Trusey Hill, where it is located, is thought to have been the site of an early monastery, and beneath the vertical set of timbers are a number of items, including a skeleton that was found on the site, and a First World War gun carriage.

Woodhenge, Barmston and distant wind turbines.

MEDIEVAL PINFOLD AT MOOT HILL, DRIFFIELD

ECHOES OF THE TOWN'S DISTANT PAST

Fine Victorian churches, commercial buildings and a splendid canal-side warehouse feature among a range of buildings that provide clues to Driffield's earlier phases of prosperity.

Moot Hill was the meeting place for members of the local assembly in the Saxon period, and at the foot of this slope is a relic from medieval times: curving brick walls mark the perimeter of a pinfold where stray animals were held until their owners claimed them. Restoration work was carried out in 1973, but a backdrop of modern housing, together with spreading shrubs on the brickwork, make it hardly recognisable as a pinfold.

Another link with earlier times is the New Year's Day custom of 'scrambling' – when local children traditionally marched down Driffield's main street while reciting rhymes and requesting favours. Shopkeepers threw coins and gifts for the children to retrieve from the roadway.

Access

Driffield is 26 miles from York and 5 miles from Bridlington via the A166.

Medieval pinfold at Moot Hill, Driffield.

ST NICHOLAS' CHURCH, HORNSEA

CRYPT WITH DUBIOUS CONNECTIONS

Access

St Nicholas'
Church is in
the centre of
Hornsea.

Relatively few churches have a crypt but those that do exist often have interesting associations. The crypt of St Nicholas' Church at Hornsea has two rooms and one of these has a fireplace built into the wall. This may be linked with the days when a reclusive elderly woman, Nanny Cankerneedle, lived in this subterranean setting.

Parts of the church date from the fourteenth and fifteenth centuries but the fabric was heavily restored in 1865-7 by Sir G.G. Scott. The tower is faced with cobbles from the beach and topped with battlements and pinnacles. Originally it had a spire but a violent storm in the mid-eighteenth century brought it crashing down.

St Nicholas'
Church,
Hornsea.

According to reports, the verger was making illicit use of the crypt to store contraband goods when the dramatic collapse took place. He took this to be a sign of God's wrath and became incurably ill. In recent times the crypt has been used to store church items.

ST MARTIN'S CHURCH, LOWTHORPE

RARE DESIGNS IN STONE

There is a real sense of mystery and romance surrounding St Martin's Church at Lowthorpe, near Driffield. Close to woodland, on the outskirts of the village, access to the church is along an avenue of evergreens.

The tower is probably fifteenth century but the church's importance dates from the previous century when it was given collegiate status with a rector and six priests to serve at six chantries.

Curiously, the roofless chancel is now blocked off from the nave and it is here, in the aisleless nave, that we come across a most unusual item of stonework.

A gravestone with a thickness of about 1ft shows a man and woman under a coverlet, with a tree spreading downwards from their shoulders to their feet and branches running sideways across their bodies. At the end of each branch is a face, seven on the man's side and six on the woman's – probably representing their thirteen children. A number of shields are spread among the roots of the tree and it seems most likely that the monument represents Sir Thomas Heslerton, who set up the chantry in 1364.

St Martin's Church, Lowthorpe.

Gravestone at St Martin's Church.

Nave of St Martin's Church.

SLEDMERE AND THE SYKES FAMILY

AN ASSORTMENT OF ELABORATE MONUMENTS

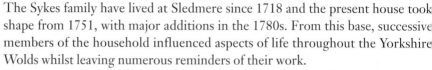

Access

Sledmere is
17 miles from
Bridlington via
the B1253 or
8 miles from
Driffield via the
B1252.

Eleanor
Cross,
Sledmere.

The Sykes family have lived at Sledmere since 1718 and the present house took shape from 1751, with major additions in the 1780s. From this base, successive members of the household influenced aspects of life throughout the Yorkshire Wolds whilst leaving numerous reminders of their work.

Opposite the pair of East Lodges is a monument to Sir Christopher Sykes, who died in 1801 after overseeing a lifetime of agricultural improvements. It was some thirty-nine years later before the village well was given a classical rotunda of Tuscan columns with lead-covered dome in memory of Sir Christopher's outstanding achievements.

Two very different stone monuments are set in open ground towards the west side of the village. In 1895 Sir Tatton Sykes employed the well-known designer, Temple Moore, to set up a copy of the crosses that were erected by King Edward I for his beloved Queen Eleanor. From a stepped base it soars some 16ft skywards, while the lower level has a wealth of detail.

Within canopied niches are statues of robed saints, and the panels on the lowest section are filled with brass portraits. After the First World War these were adapted as a memorial to twenty-three local men who were lost in action.

A short distance away, again on a short flight of steps, is a most unusual stone monument. The Waggoners' Memorial was fashioned by Carlo Magnoni to Sir Mark Sykes' design and has a massive central column surrounded by four peripheral shafts. It celebrates the role played by the 1,200 men of the Waggoners' Reserve in the First World War. Formed in 1912 after a call from Lt-Col. Sir Mark Sykes, they were called up two years later and provided transport for British Expeditionary Forces on the Western Front.

Carvings on the central column show Waggoners leaving their farmsteads and crossing the English Channel to link up with the battle front. An indication of the depth of anti-German feeling at that time is apparent, with German troops shown in grotesquely distorted parodies whilst involved in barbarous acts of savagery, compared with the calm dignity of their English foes. The last surviving member of the Waggoners' Reserve died in 1993.

Three miles south of Sledmere village, on Garton Hill, the rolling landscape is dominated by the outlines of the Sir Tatton Sykes Memorial Tower. Designed by J. Gibbs, an Oxford-based architect, it measures 120ft in height and has brown and red stonework that is visible for several miles around. It was

Waggoners'
Memorial,
Sledmere.

Sir Tatton
Sykes
Memorial
Tower.

completed in 1865, two years after the death of Sir Tatton Sykes, and resembles
a tall pyramid. Around the base are carved panels, with a pastoral scene depicting
a hillside farm, neighbouring sheep fields, and an illustration of Sir Tatton
Sykes riding his horse. Upper sections are covered with projecting stonework,
enclosing highly decorative windows that offer views across the Sykes estates to
the North Sea coast.

GARROWBY

BELL-SHAPED BOUNDARY MARKERS OF THE CLASSICAL VARIETY

Access

The roadside 'bells' are on the south side of the A166, close to the summit of Garrowby Hill.

Dotted at intervals along roadside verges on the A166, near Garrowby Hill, are a number of puzzling concrete 'bells'. Close inspection reveals that they are inscribed with Roman words and numerals, which offer clues to their purpose.

Two 'bells' on the A166 carry the lettering 'EBORACUM' and 'VIAXX' which may indicate the road to York and the distance involved. Another pair, showing 'ACER ARVUM', could be taken to denote farmland with fertile ground. The agricultural theme is continued with 'bells' marked LARGUS LINGUA – luxuriant 'tongue' of land.

Among others that may be spotted along the main road and side lanes leading to Millington are LIMES and TRAMES, suggesting a boundary path and side path.

Local knowledge reveals that these mysterious roadside features were positioned here forty years ago by a farmer from Wold House Farm, who chose an unusual, if not unique, way of marking the perimeter of his land.

Boundary marker at Garrowby.

HOLME-UPON-SPALDING MOOR'S LOCK-UP

SMALL, CIRCULAR PLACE OF DETENTION

Access

Workhouse Farm is about a mile south of Holme-upon-Spalding Moor on the A614 to Howden.

A short, circular brick tower close to Workhouse Farm at Holme-upon-Spalding Moor hardly warrants a second glance, but in fact it represents a grim link with the poor and needy of the Victorian era.

Under the terms of the Poor Law Amendment Act of 1834, outdoor relief was abolished and parishes were grouped into unions with a central workhouse. There was great opposition to these institutions, or 'Bastilles' as they became known, but before 1840 ⁵⁄₇ of the population of England and Wales lived in areas covered by unions.

Conditions were usually harsh, with families dispersed to different areas of the building, very basic meals and menial, repetitive tasks for the inmates, yet this method of providing for the poor and needy members of society endured until the 1940s. Many former workhouse buildings have survived after adaptation for a different use.

The simple tower at Workhouse Farm is believed to have been a lock-up that served the adjacent workhouse building; its high walls and small slit windows must have offered a grim prospect for any miscreants.

Former lock-up at Holme-upon-Spalding Moor.

LAND OF NOD

AN UNLIKELY PLACE NAME

A roadside sign, about a mile south of Holme-upon-Spalding Moor, gives directions to this unlikely location which conjures up images from fairytales. In reality, the long, straight lane leads to a small group of farm buildings backing onto the Market Weighton Canal and we are left to speculate about the origins of this place name.

Access

The Land of Nod lies at the end of the lane that runs east from the A614, about a mile south of Holme-upon-Spalding.

Land of Nod signpost.

ST MICHAEL AND ALL ANGELS, GARTON-ON-THE-WOLDS

AN INCREDIBLE INTERIOR OF BIBLICAL EPISODES

Access

Garton-on-the-Wolds is about 3 miles north-west of Driffield via the A166.

A number of East Yorkshire's churches benefited from charitable treatment by Sir Tatton Sykes of Sledmere, including the Church of St Michael and All Angels at Garton-on-the-Wolds.

At first glance the exterior has many Norman style features but the interior reveals an abundance of black-and-white mosaics (with a touch of yellow).

The wall decorations were designed for Sir Tatton Sykes by G.E. Street and include a whole pageant of biblical characters such as martyrs, apostles, saints and angels. There are scenes depicting the Creation and the Garden of Eden, the building of the Ark, the return of Joseph from Egypt, the Nativity and a doom scene showing St Michael separating the saved from the lost.

These splendid illustrations are in the thirteenth-century style but hold clear indications of the Victorian era. Overall they represent an amazing display of biblical episodes and their importance was highlighted with restoration in commemoration of Nikolaus Pevsner, the architectural historian who died in 1983.

One of the mosaics in
St Michael and All Angels,
Garton-on-the-Wolds.

SEATON ROSS SUNDIAL

A TIMEPIECE ON THE GRAND SCALE

Sundials are fairly commonplace in rural settings – most often seen on churches and prominent public buildings – but few, if any, can match the dimensions of the huge timepiece on the front wall of Dial Hall Farm at Seaton Ross.

    The white-painted half circle, which spreads across the centre of the farm's upper storey with its lowest point just above the front doorway, was the work of William Watson, who lived locally from 1784 to 1857. There is another example of these giant dials about a mile away on the village's main street. Measuring 12ft in diameter, it extends from the eaves around the upper window and almost touches the lower window.

Access

Seaton Ross is 10 miles west of Market Weighton via the A1079

Sundial on Dial Hall Farm, Seaton Ross.

Sundial on a property in Main Street, Seaton Ross.

In contrast, St Edmund's Church has a much smaller dial with the date 1823 above the main entrance. Just a few feet away, close to the pathway, is the gravestone of Margaret Harper, who died in 1853. Mistrusted and ill-treated by fellow villagers, her headstone carries a trenchant riposte:

The faults you've seen in me strive to
   avoid
Search your own hearts and you'll be
   well employed.

Grave of Margaret Harper,
Seaton Ross.

St Edmund's
Church,
Seaton Ross.

Access

Melbourne is about 7 miles south-west of Pocklington via Allerthorpe. The former church is at the end of St Monica's Close.

MELBOURNE CHURCH

QUAINT APPEAL OF THE FORMER 'TIN TABERNACLE'

Church buildings take many forms and, in some areas, a rapid growth in population often resulted in construction of a temporary place of worship. A number of these simple structures were built from sheets of corrugated iron and consequently acquired the name 'tin tabernacle'. Although most have been replaced in recent years there is a delightful example of such a church at Melbourne, about 7 miles from Pocklington. Built in 1882 on the outskirts of

he village, there are echoes of the Australian outback among the encircling
reenery, but it is the captivating features of the grade II listed church that hold
most interest.

Decorative barge boards and tall, lancet-style windows are dominated by a
orch turret set in the area between transept and nave, while grey painted walls
nd a red roof and steeple add to the overall allure.

In recent years the building has ceased to operate as a church and is now a
rivate residence.

ormer 'tin tabernacle', Melbourne.

WILLIAM BRADLEY OF MARKET WEIGHTON

TALLEST RECORDED ENGLISHMAN

orn in Market Weighton in February 1787, William Bradley lived a simple
xistence up to his death in 1820 at the age of thirty-three. It seems that there
as nothing out of the ordinary about his lifestyle and it is simply Bradley's
mormous stature that singles him out for attention.

He weighed 14lbs at birth and reached a height of 7ft 9in by the age of
ineteen – by which time he tipped the scales at an incredible 27 stone. During
is lifetime William Bradley made a good living by parading his enormous
ulk at fairgrounds and shows, where he was heralded as the 'tallest man ever
ecorded in England'.

Access

Market
Weighton
is 19 miles
south-east of
York via the
A1079.

On his death he was given a secret burial in the churchyard of All Saints' Church, but fears that body snatchers might remove Bradley's mortal remains led to an exhumation and reburial inside the parish church.

Market Weighton's pride in their local giant is illustrated by a number of features around the town's streets. A plaque measuring 15in in length and 5½in in width – the size of his footprint – is set on the wall of the house on York Road where William Bradley lived. A room inside the building has a full-length painting copied from an etching.

Close by, a life-sized statue of William Bradley gazes down the narrow High Street. It is sculpted from the trunk of an oak tree that was estimated to be more than 200 years old – which means that it would have been growing during the giant's lifetime.

In recent years a series of twenty-three giant granite footprints have been set in pavements around the town to create the Giant Bradley Heritage Trail, and an annual Giant Bradley Day offers the chance to celebrate the town's best-known character.

Curiously, the nearby village of Shiptonthorpe was the birthplace of Edwin Calvert who never grew more than 36in and died at the age of just seventeen from excessive alcohol consumption.

Life-sized statue of William Bradley.

Left: Plaques relating to William Bradley.

Right: All Saints' Church, Market Weighton.

ALL SAINTS' CHURCH, POCKLINGTON AND 'THE FLYING MAN'

TRAGIC OUTCOME OF A DARING STUNT

Long before the days of modern aviators and pioneering flights, Thomas Pelling performed his dramatic airborne stunt at locations throughout the country. His act involved a 'flight' from a high point to ground level using fabricated wings tied to his arms and legs, with one ankle secured to a pulley suspended from a rope.

At Pocklington the chosen high point was the church tower and the rope ended at a windlass set in the ground some distance away. On 10 April 1773, a large crowd gathered to witness Pelling's amazing performance – but sadly the planned routine misfired.

As the rope loosened, Henry Pelling was hurled to his death against the church wall. A memorial plaque on the external wall of the chancel records details of his extraordinary and tragic accident.

Access

Pocklington is 16 miles from Driffield and 14 miles from York on the north side of the A1079.

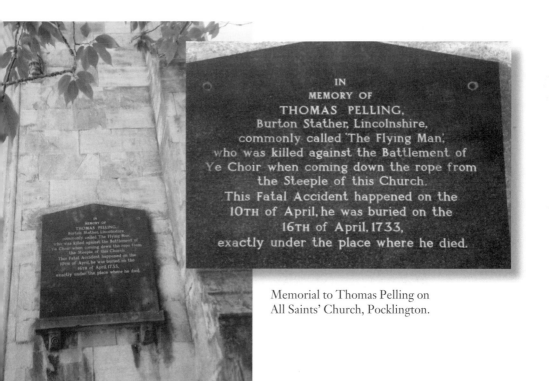

IN
MEMORY OF
THOMAS PELLING,
Burton Stather, Lincolnshire,
commonly called 'The Flying Man',
who was killed against the Battlement of
Ye Choir when coming down the rope from
the Steeple of this Church.
This Fatal Accident happened on the
10TH of April, he was buried on the
16TH of April, 1733,
exactly under the place where he died.

Memorial to Thomas Pelling on All Saints' Church, Pocklington.

MILLINGTON'S AGRICULTURAL LINKS

... OF 'GAITS' AND CARTWHEELS

Access

Millington
village is
3 miles
north-east of
Pocklington.

Millington's origins are thought to reach back to the Roman era when
settlement known as Delgovicia flourished because of its closeness to water from
natural springs. Today the long-distance route of the Wolds Way, which passe
through the village and nearby ancient ash woodland, has been designated as
Site of Special Scientific Interest.

Millington Pastures were granted to the parish by Act of Parliament in 177
during the enclosure movement. At this time, pasture land was allocated o
'stinted' out to farmers in 'gaits' – an amount of grazing land for a stipulate
number of sheep – and the number of 'gaits' given to each farmer corresponde
with the amount of land that he held in the parish before enclosure took place.

The village inn on the main street has the uncommon name of 'The Gate'
which may well be derived from the word 'gait', as in grazing land. One of th
inn's rooms has an extraordinary feature – a map of the local area that cover
much of the ceiling.

A roadside object close to Town Farm has probably perplexed and intrigue
passers-by for many years. A metal wheel attached to a vertical stanchion wa
used as a 'hooping iron' to shape cartwheels and serves as a reminder of th
village's earlier importance as an agricultural settlement.

Map on the
ceiling of
The Gate at
Millington.

THE KIPLINGCOTES DERBY

ENGLAND'S OLDEST HORSE RACE

There is no sign of the village of Kiplingcotes in the rolling countryside to the east of Pocklington, yet this quiet setting stages this country's longest established horse race.

Tradition suggests that the race originated in the fifteenth century but the official date – 1519 – is displayed on the finishing post that is set in a roadside verge close to Warter. The race has been run over the same course, on the third Thursday in March, since the first outing and it has a most unusual set of rules and regulations.

The race starts at midday following a unique weigh-in that is held at the winning post. Male and female riders must weigh at least ten stone and if extra weight is required it must be carried on the person rather than the saddle. An old stone post set in the roadside verge marks the starting point for this unique race that runs over fields, a railway bridge, along country lanes and down stretches of metalled roadway.

Prize money was initially organised by Lord Burlington and a small number of landed gentry, who raised the sum of £365. The winner traditionally received interest from the total sum with the runner-up taking the entry fees, but as this usually meant that second place was better rewarded, a fixed first prize has recently been introduced.

Access

The village of Warter is 5 miles east of Pocklington on the B1246. From Warter the post is about 3 miles to the south in a roadside verge.

ST EDITH'S CHURCH, BISHOP WILTON

INCREDIBLE VICTORIAN DESIGN WORK

Many of East Yorkshire's churches show the influence of Sir Tatton Sykes' generosity during the late nineteenth century, but it is probably seen nowhere better than at St Edith's Church, Bishop Wilton.

Aspects of work from the Norman period and the thirteenth and fourteenth centuries remain in the nave and chancel, but the splendid hammer-beam roof and remarkable floor date from Sykes' phase of restoration (1858-9).

J.L. Pearson and Temple Moore were foremost in designing these eye-catching features from the roof, with its range of colours and gold leaf work, to the black-and-white marble mosaic floor. A pattern of scrolls swirls around all manner of birds created by Salviati in a display that was copied from the floor of the Vatican. The original inspiration for this splendid feature is said to have been the Palace of the Caesars in Rome.

Completing this powerful setting is a finely carved font, and cover, showing figures of saints.

Access

Bishop Wilton is 6 miles east of Stamford Bridge via A166 and south of Garrowby Hill.

The floor of St Edith's
Church, Bishop
Wilton.

St Edith's Church,
Bishop Wilton.

LONDESBOROUGH

A VILLAGE WITH AN ILLUSTRIOUS PAST

Londesborough's position in a sheltered valley of Easthorpe Wold, close to the East Beck, accounts for its ancient origins and subsequent continuous occupation. There is evidence of a Roman township – Delgovitia – in the locality and tradition suggests that King Edwin had a palace close by. Centuries later, ownership of this area passed to the Clifford family, then the Earls of Burlington and the Cavendish family, before it was sold to George Hudson, the 'Railway King'. More recently it was held by the Denison family, who took the name Londesborough for the title of their peerage.

There are links with many of these early families and individuals in the Church of All Saints and around the village in buildings such as the school, almshouses and concert hall. The concert hall, on Top Street, began life as the estate laundry and is believed to have been completed in time for a royal visit, probably in 1882. It was certainly used to stage the cricket club ball, in 1889, and the children's tea party in 1891.

Access

Londesborough is 3 miles north of Market Weighton.

Interior of the concert hall, Londesborough.

Murals on the wall of the concert hall.

A curious feature of the concert hall is the artwork on internal walls, which was completed during 1945 by two German prisoners of war. They were transported from their camp at Storwood to Londesborough each day and made paintbrushes for their work from their own hair. The paintings may appear to be rather theatrical and stylised but the various Georgian or Regency scenes, along with a view of Londesborough Hall, hold enormous interest.

WHARRAM PERCY

FASCINATING INSIGHT INTO ASPECTS OF EARLIER VILLAGE LIFE

Wharram Percy ranks as the best preserved of this country's 3,500 deserted villages and, since 1950, systematic excavations and analysis have revealed fascinating details of life in this remote rural community.

The earliest houses at Wharram Percy date from the Iron Age (around 100 BC) and there is evidence of continuous occupation by Roman and Saxon settlers, as well as their medieval counterparts.

Today the site is dominated by the ruins of St Martin's Church, which has stonework dating from the eleventh, twelfth and thirteenth centuries. During the early 1990s, some 700 human skeletons were removed from beneath the

Access

Wharram Percy lies midway between York and Scarborough and is 7 miles south-east of Malton via the B1248.

St Martin's Church, Wharram Percy.

floor of the church and scientific analysis revealed that half of the eleventh to fifteenth-century population reached the age of fifty. Many of the women's skeletons showed signs of osteoporosis – which was previously believed to be a twentieth-century condition.

The stream running through Wharram was an important resource for the community and the southern aspect is dominated by a pond which began as a small millpond serving a Saxon corn mill. A block of sandstone recovered from the pond had been carved with markings for playing 'nine men's morris' and speculation suggests that it could have been fashioned by one of the masons working on the nearby church building, for use during a rest break.

At its peak in the early stages of the fourteenth century, Wharram Percy was made up of thirty families (giving a population of about 150), but by 1435 there were only sixteen households and seventy years later the last villagers had left.

Many factors contributed to Wharram Percy's demise – including outbreaks of plague and conversion of large tracts of land for sheep farming – but St Martin's Church continued to be used by villagers from nearby Thixendale until 1870. The last regular service took place in 1949, but scientific research of human remains from the area of the church and adjacent village continue to provide insight into aspects of life and death in a medieval community.

BATTLE OF STAMFORD BRIDGE
A SMALL MONUMENT WITH MAJOR SIGNIFICANCE

Access

Stamford Bridge is 7 miles from York on the A166 and the monument is on the north side of the road in the centre of the township.

The significance of many of this country's major battlefields is often easily recalled – Hastings (Senlac Hill) in 1066 and Bosworth Field in 1485, among others – but the importance of the Battle of Stamford Bridge in September 1066 may be overlooked.

A simple memorial stone in the centre of the village (close to the A166) states in both English and Norwegian that 'The Battle of Stamford Bridge was fought in this vicinity on the 25 September 1066' and an obelisk was added some years later. The battle saw English forces, under Harold of Wessex, defeat invading Scandinavian raiders, led by Tostig and Hardraada [sic], to effectively end North European hopes of seizing territory in this country.

Almost within hours of his victory at Stamford Bridge, news reached Harold of another invading army. This time the threat was on the south coast in the

Monument for the Battle of Stamford Bridge.

Plaque relating to the Battle of Stamford Bridge.

shape of French troops under William of Normandy, and battle-weary English forces had to begin the long march southwards.

Speculation suggests that if the Battle of Stamford Bridge had not taken place, Harold's army would have reached Hastings fresh, rather than weary from a recent battle, and the Normans could have been defeated. If Hardraada [*sic*] had triumphed at Stamford Bridge he would have taken control of the North Country while invading Normans established themselves in southern areas. In that case, this country could well have been made up of a Norwegian province in the north and a French region in the south, with little prospect of a nation of England.

Considering this possible outcome, the simple roadside monument in Stamford Bridge assumes much greater importance.

three

City of York

YORK COLD WAR BUNKER
HIGHLY UNUSUAL RECENT MILITARY STRUCTURE

Access

York Cold
War Bunker is
about a mile
from the city
centre, close to
Acomb Road
and near the
Carlton Tavern.

The City of York is renowned for its numerous phases of military and civilian occupation and this rich vein of heritage extends into recent times in the form of a Cold War bunker.

'No. 20 Group Royal Observer HQ' is a semi-sunken shelter which would have monitored nuclear explosions and fallout in the Yorkshire area during the Cold War era. The bunker was constructed in 1961, a year before the Cuban Missile Crisis, and remained operational until 1991. It represented one of twenty-nine bases throughout the United Kingdom that were operated by the

Information board
for York Cold War
Bunker.

Above & below: York Cold War Bunker.

United Kingdom Warning and Monitoring Organisation (UKWMO) and manned by the Royal Observer Corps.

Following agreement on a non-aggression treaty between NATO and Warsaw Pact Countries, the bunker was decommissioned in 1991 but a recent programme of restoration has seen it reopened for public visits under the management of English Heritage. Tours of this highly unusual property include visits to the officers' room, telephone exchange, kitchen, dormitories, operations room and decontamination areas.

WHIP-MA-WHOP-MA-GATE

A LENGTHY NAME FOR YORK'S SHORTEST STREET

Access

Whip-Ma-Whop-Ma-Gate is outside St Crux Parish Room between Pavement and Colliergate

The Shambles must rate as York's best-known thoroughfare but a neighbouring roadway, Whip-Ma-Whop-Ma-Gate, surely has the city's strangest street name.

A roadside plaque explains that this is indeed the shortest street in York and was known in 1505 as 'Whitnourwhatnourgate', meaning 'what a street'. Another explanation of the name suggests that it was the location where felons used to be whipped and whopped.

Today it is a busy link route from Pavement and The Stonebow to Colliergate, with a footpath paved in York stone by York Civic Trust in 1984.

Signpost for Whip-Ma-Whop-Ma-Gate.

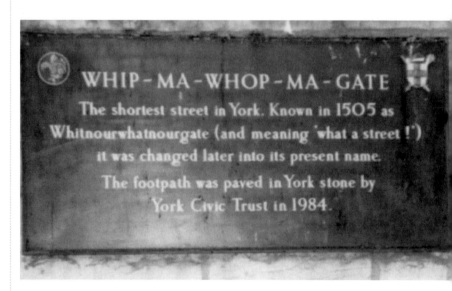

Whip-Ma-Whop-Ma-Gate plaque.

AN ICEHOUSE

A DEEP, COOL STORAGE PLACE

Situated close to the city walls and adjacent to Monk Bar is a curious rounded brick building. With an arched entrance and bulbous sides it has the appearance of a kiln or mine entrance – it is, in fact, an icehouse.

Icehouses were mainly built in the eighteenth and nineteenth centuries to store ice that had been gathered from a nearby river or pond. Construction of the house was important if the ice was to remain frozen; it was usually built into a slope, so that any melted water could flow out of the bottom. A group of trees, or in this case the city walls, would provide shade and help to keep the internal temperature low.

Access to the insulated pit was through a small tunnel in the dome, with at least two sets of doors to keep the interior cool and an air vent to reduce damp (which accelerated melting).

Ice that was gathered for storage was not particularly pure and was only used to cool bottles or place in iceboxes. Although refrigerators were introduced in the late nineteenth century, many icehouses continued in use well into the twentieth century.

This intriguing icehouse dates from about 1800 and stored ice that would have been gathered from the River Foss about 300 yards away.

Access

The icehouse is close to Monk Bar and overlooks St Maurice's Road.

Icehouse close to Monk Bar, York.

NUMBERS 20-22 FOSSGATE

FABULOUS FAÇADE IN A STREET OF NOBLE FRONTAGES

Access

Fossgate runs
between The
Stonebow and
Pavement and
Walmgate on
the other side
of the River
Foss.

Fossgate has an assortment of fine frontages, including the splendid gatehouse of the Merchant Adventurers' Hall, but the boldest façade by far belongs to a twentieth-century former cinema building.

Built in 1911 to designs by W.H. Whincup, this ground floor entrance to the Electric Theatre is enriched with classical features. A huge central alcove is supported by four Ionic-style columns and a covering of cream-coloured glazed tiles is highlighted with garlands of fruit. Topping the alcove is a large human head with its mouth open as if smiling or perhaps snarling. In view of the building's earlier use as a cinema, surely it must be a guffaw of laughter!

Numbers 20-22 Fossgate,
York.

THE BLUE BELL, FOSSGATE

SMALL BUT FULL OF CHARACTER

The City of York has numerous places of refreshment and each one has its own distinctive features and compelling tales. My own favourite – The Blue Bell – is tucked away from the bustle of central streets on Fossgate.

Built as an inn during 1798 on the site of two medieval properties, this hostelry rates as York's smallest public house and originally the rear of the building backed onto Fossgate. At that time the frontage overlooked Lady Peckett's Yard, located between Fossgate and Piccadilly, but it was the influential Rowntree family that engineered the inn's realignment in its present position.

Access

The Blue Bell inn is located in Fossgate.

The Blue Bell, Fossgate, York.

The Rowntree company, makers of chocolate products, was founded in 1862 by Henry Isaac Rowntree. Benjamin Rowntree (1871-1954) became well known as a sociologist and philanthropist through wide-ranging surveys of working-class living conditions in York.

The Blue Bell inn assumed its present form in 1903 and, although the central serving area is a more recent addition, many of the original fittings have been retained. This splendidly compact, atmospheric inn was owned by the Robinson family for more than sixty years and for a number of years York City Football Club held their board meetings in the room at the rear of the building. (The club was admitted to the Football League in 1926.)

From its early days there are lurid reports of cruel sports such as cock fighting held here, but during the Second World War it served a more charitable purpose as a soup kitchen. Women were banned from the public bar until about 1990 but nowadays there is a warm welcome for everyone in this fascinating two-roomed hostelry.

Interior of The Blue Bell.

The bar of The Blue Bell.

BARCLAYS BANK BUILDING, PARLIAMENT STREET

SPLENDID CENTRE OF COMMERCE

The streets of York are filled with buildings of historic interest from many eras and it is easy to overlook some fine structures of more recent vintage.

Barclays Bank, at the junction of High Ousegate and Parliament Street, must rate as one of the city's finest commercial buildings, yet its intricate external features often remain unnoticed. Designed by E. Kirby of Liverpool and completed in 1901, its red brickwork rises from a base of polished stonework to incorporate an array of patterns around gargoyles, square and rounded windows and a highly ornate arch above the main entrance.

Without doubt it is a building to savour.

Access

Barclays Bank is on the corner of High Ousegate and Parliament Street.

Barclays Bank building, Parliament Street, York.

SHAMBLES

CHARMING, COLOURFUL AND SO NARROW

Access

Shambles
runs between
Pavement and
King's Court.

York's best-known thoroughfare derives its name from its earlier importance as the long-established centre of the butchery trade. Post-war modernisation and renovation of properties in this narrowest of roadways has reduced the range of authentic frontages; however, much fine timber framing and dipping floor levels on projecting sections preserve its enduring charm.

Upper storeys extend so far across the lane that it is possible to shake hands with a person in the opposite property. No. 35 houses a shrine to St Margaret Clitherow, who was martyred for her Roman Catholic beliefs.

Shambles, York.

MONK BAR

THE TALLEST OF THE CITY'S ENTRY POINTS

A walk around York's city walls opens up fine views of the minster and other central aspects, as well as allowing visitors to take in the bars that formed entrance points to the medieval settlement. The walls encircle York for almost 3 miles and represent the longest and best-preserved example in this country.

Monk Bar is the tallest of York's gateways, with ground to second floors completed in the fourteenth century and the third added in the fifteenth century. A portcullis is housed on the first floor, with its winding mechanism on the second, and at third floor level a walkway connects rounded turrets topped with stone figures.

A barbican was removed from the Bar in about 1825 and between 1845 and 1913 it was used as a house. In recent times, the upper rooms of Monk Bar have accommodated the Richard III Museum.

Access

Monk Bar is at the junction of Monkgate, Lord Mayor's Walk and St Maurice's Road.

Monk Bar, York.

80

RED DEVIL AND ASSORTED CHARACTERS

ADDING COLOUR AND INTEREST TO CENTRAL STREETS

Access

Stonegate runs
from Petergate
to St Helen's
Square.
Low Petergate
links High
Petergate with
Colliergate.
Coney Street
joins St
Helen's Square
and High
Ousegate.

York probably has a greater array of decorative features on houses and shops than any other town or city centre in the country. The best known of these curious characters must be the 'red devil' that is perched below the first floor overhang of No. 33 in Stonegate. Close by, in Coffee Yard, were the premises where the city's first newspaper, the *York Mercury*, was printed from 1719, and the children working there became known as 'little devils'. The red devil – complete with

Red devil, Stonegate.

Red Indian, Low Petergate.

Britannia, on the junction of High Petergate and Minster Gates.

horns and cloven hoofs – is said to have got the blame when things went wrong and it was also believed to be unlucky to look him in the eye.

Round the corner, in Low Petergate, a Red Indian, complete with headdress and full skirt, stands proudly above No. 74a. It is the traditional sign for a tobacconist shop and although it was stolen a few years ago, this fine fellow is now back in pride of place.

The most elegant of these tiny figures is the little admiral who stands on top of the clock outside St Martin's Church in Coney Street. Complete with neat blue and gold tailcoat and tricorne hat, white waistcoat, breeches and stockings, he was fashioned in the eighteenth century.

During an air raid of 1942 the church was destroyed and the clock face needed replacing, but the proud admiral remained stubbornly intact.

HOLY TRINITY CHURCH

A CAPTIVATING PLACE OF WORSHIP

Access

Holy Trinity Church is located on the west side of Goodramgate.

In many ways York's old churches are overshadowed by the minster, but each place of worship holds interest and appeal.

Tucked away behind tiny shops is the quirky Church of Holy Trinity, which has many quaint and captivating features. The exterior roofs slope at different levels while internal walls and arcades are leaning. Uneven floors are so irregular that the rare Jacobean box pews dip at all sorts of angles and the old three-decker pulpit (now reduced to two decks) rises among them. Other unusual features include a sunken chapel on the south side of the chancel and another on the south side of the nave.

The variations in the building are probably explained by the different phases of construction. The earliest sections of the church date from the Norman period, with additions in the thirteenth and fourteenth centuries, and a particularly captivating feature is the fifteenth-century glass in the east window.

Gold, blue and purple colours predominate as the top level shows St George and the dragon, John the Baptist, the Trinity, St John and St Christopher with the Madonna and her parents, and St Ursula protecting a group of maidens, spreading along the lower level.

It comes as little surprise that Holy Trinity often features in reports of ghostly sightings.

Holy Trinity Church, Goodramgate, York.

LADY ROW, GOODRAMGATE

OLDEST SURVIVING HOUSES

A short row of houses in Goodramgate – known as Lady Row – represent York's oldest surviving houses. Built in about 1320 for chantry priests, their low timber-framed construction has been cited as the earliest example in the whole country.

The addition of new windows at first-floor level, as well as modern shop fronts, cannot hide the cottages' genuine antiquity which is most clearly shown in the dipping jettied frontage.

Access

Goodramgate links Monk Bar with Low Petergate and Colliergate.

Lady Row, Goodramgate.

UNITARIAN CHAPEL

THE FIRST NON-CONFORMIST PLACE OF WORSHIP IN YORK

Access

The Unitarian chapel is located on St Saviourgate between Spen Lane and Colliergate.

This fine chapel was completed in 1693, some four years after the Act of Toleration allowed Non-conformist places of worship to be built. It was originally Presbyterian and the project was carried out by a local resident, Lady Sarah Hewley. (This accounts for its original name of Lady Hewley's Chapel.)

It was the first large brick building in York, constructed to an unusual Greek cross design, with a soaring central tower and a spacious interior surrounded by large windows. The bricks were made from local clay and the walls were constructed in three layers and not bonded together. Top-quality bricks were used on exterior walls, next-best bricks on the inside and rougher bricks formed the middle, unseen wall which provided the main support for the heavy Westmorland slate roof.

The early church was furnished with box pews in all four arms of the chapel, with a high pulpit located at one corner of the central space. During the Victorian era, pews in the rear areas were removed and bench pews were placed in the other three arms. For some years the pews were painted a rather dark blue, before being replaced by the distinctive red that is still on display.

Unitarian chapel, St Saviourgate, York.

During the late twentieth century the building was granted grade II* listed building status. Restoration work continued into recent years, with internal repairs and redecoration followed by replacement of the slate roof and re-arrangement of interior areas.

ST MARGARET'S CHURCH, WALMGATE

AN ASSORTMENT OF MATERIALS AND STYLES IN SPLENDID HARMONY

Viewed through a set of stately cast-iron gates, the Church of St Margaret seems to be a haven amid the bustle of Walmgate, and its curious mixture of building materials adds to the attractive nature of the location.

The church tower was completed in 1684 and is mainly brickwork with stone corner supports and castellated parapet. Other parts of the church were rebuilt in 1851-2 but this fascinating building includes a Norman porch – moved from St Nicholas' Hospital on the Hull road – and other sections dating from the fourteenth century through to the 1800s.

In recent years St Margaret's Church has been tastefully adapted to accommodate the National Centre for Early Music.

Access

St Margaret's Church is on the north side of Walmgate.

St Margaret's Church, Walmgate, York.

LENDAL TOWER

MUCH-CHANGED DESIGN BUT STILL WITH A WATERY LINK

Access

Lendal Tower is adjacent to Lendal Bridge on the north side of the River Ouse.

Now overshadowed, to some extent, by the adjacent Lendal Bridge, Lendal Tower has had a chequered existence since its completion in about AD 1300. Originally it was a round tower, with similarities to the Barker Tower across the river, but during the seventeenth and eighteenth centuries Lendal Tower was given greater height and circumference.

By the 1670s it was used to pump a water supply to the city from the Ouse using horse-powered water wheels. In the 1750s the horses were replaced by a Newcomen steam engine, which was improved by the eminent civil engineer John Smeaton (1724-92) in 1784.

Further changes took place in the nineteenth century, with the replacement of wooden water pipes by cast-iron tubes during the early 1800s and removal of the steam engine in 1846. The tower was also reduced in height by 10ft and given the castellated appearance that it still displays.

A link with the earlier waterworks still remains, for in 1677 the tower was rented for this purpose for 500 years with an annual payment of one peppercorn. Accordingly, it still accommodates the York Waterworks PLC boardrooms.

Lendal Tower.

LENDAL TOWER

Dating from about 1300, it was originally part of the City's defences, with a defensive chain stretching from here to the Tower on the opposite bank. In 1677 it was leased to the predecessors of The York Waterworks Plc for five hundred years, at an annual rent of one peppercorn, for use as a water tower. During the 18th century it housed a steam pumping engine modified to the design of John Smeaton FRS, then a proprietor of the Waterworks. It ceased to be used for those purposes in 1850. In 1932 it was refurbished and now houses the Company's Board Rooms.

Lendal Tower plaque.

CENTENARY METHODIST CHAPEL

A MIGHTY PLACE OF WORSHIP

Up and down the country Methodist places of worship vary in size from humble Primitive Methodist chapels to grander town structures, but there are few remaining examples of the very large chapels of the mid-nineteenth century.

York's Centenary Methodist Chapel was built in 1840 to mark 100 years since the birth of Methodism. Designed by James Simpson of Leeds, it was intended to represent a cathedral of Methodism and its simple design, on such a majestic scale, makes a very powerful statement.

The frontage has four huge Ionic order columns supporting a plain pediment while pale brickwork is relieved by stone pilasters. Within the building, a horseshoe-shaped interior includes a gallery, supported by nine Corinthian columns, and an organ, made in 1841 by John Brown of York, which is said to be one of the finest in the city.

The Centenary Methodist Chapel has grade II listed building status and retains a number of interesting features, including a coffered ceiling decorated with acanthus leaf bosses, a window in the gallery containing the original ruby, orange and blue flashed glass, and a fine pulpit of Spanish mahogany (which was reduced in height by 10ft to its present dimensions in the 1960s).

Access

Centenary Methodist Chapel is located on St Saviourgate.

Centenary Methodist Chapel.

THE OBSERVATORY

A WHIMSICAL BASE FOR VIEWING THE HEAVENS

Access

The observatory is within the Museum Gardens between Museum Street and Marygate.

York's Museum Gardens cover 10 acres and were established by members of the Yorkshire Philosophical Society in 1822. Within the grounds are the ruins of a medieval hospital and St Mary's Abbey, the Roman Multangular Tower and the Yorkshire Museum, as well as the curious outlines of a small observatory.

It was constructed by the Yorkshire Philosophical Society during 1832-3 and included a revolving roof developed by John Smeaton. Space within the observatory was intended to accommodate instruments donated to the society by Dr Pearson, rector of South Kilworth in Leicestershire.

Surrounded by greenery, there is a whimsical air around the observatory – but its importance was recognised in 1981. A tablet on the building explains that it was refurbished to celebrate the 150th anniversary of the British Association's meeting in York and was opened by the Association's president, HRH The Duke of Kent.

Observatory, York.

WALMGATE BAR

A UNIQUE FORTIFIED ENTRY POINT

Each of York's bars has its own characteristics and point of interest; Walmgate Bar holds particular significance as the only town gate in England to have retained is barbican.

There is mention of fortifications at Walmgate in the mid-twelfth century but the present structure was completed some 200 years later. External sections of the Bar were damaged during artillery bombardment in 1644 but were soon repaired after the Civil War. On the inward (city) side of the Bar, a homely-looking building is rather older than might first appear. Standing on two Tuscan columns and including sets of windows on two floor levels, it was added to the earlier stonework in 1580 and is topped by a decorative balustrade.

Access

Walmgate Bar is at the southern end of Walmgate where the A1079 road joins Barbican Road and Foss Islands Road.

Walmgate Bar.

CLIFFORD'S TOWER

CHEQUERED HISTORY OF AN UNUSUAL STRUCTURE

Access

Clifford's
Tower is
adjacent to
Tower Street
on a site
between the
River Ouse
and River Foss.

William the Conqueror's forces built two castles at York during the late eleventh century. One stood on the Old Bailey near Skeldergate Bridge and the other was erected on the mount, now covered by Clifford's Tower. The timber structure that preceded Clifford's Tower was the setting for a terrible event on 16 March 1190 when roughly 150 Jews, who had gathered there for safety, took their own lives rather than face an angry mob.

Clifford's Tower was built between 1250 and 1275 to a plan that is unique in England and it derives its name from the first governor. Clearance of land around the mount in the mid-1900s has given this curious stronghold even greater prominence.

Reached by a flight of fifty-five steps, it rises about 40ft above the top of the mound and has the shape of a quatrefoil, with a front section that was added in the seventeenth century. The walls are 9ft thick with two staircases, fireplaces and a well, along with unusual windows which have normal upper halves that become arrow slits in the lower section.

From the fourteenth to sixteenth centuries the tower served as a prison, but in the 1590s the stonework was being dismantled until the city council saved it. Half a century later it was adapted as a barracks and continued in use from the Civil War period, for Royalist troops, through to the reign of Charles II.

Following a fire in 1684 it became a decorative skyline feature and was then enclosed within the adjacent prison complex before being taken over by English Heritage in recent years.

Clifford's Tower.

DICK TURPIN'S GRAVE

FINAL RESTING PLACE OF A NOTORIOUS ROBBER

A quiet public garden close to Fishergate's Bar and Tower was formerly a churchyard linked with St George's medieval church. Any trace of the church building was removed during the eighteenth century, but included among a number of tombstones that are spread out around the open space is one for John Palmer, 'otherwise known as Richard Turpin, the notorious highwayman and horse stealer'.

Born in Essex in about 1705, Turpin trained as a butcher and soon supplemented his supply of meat by stealing sheep, cattle and deer from local farmers. During 1734 he joined a band of robbers known as the Essex Gang who carried out raids on isolated properties. Such was their notoriety that a reward of £100 was offered for the capture of a gang member and Turpin switched his criminal activities to the Cambridge area.

With an associate named Tom King, Turpin carried out robberies in Cambridge, Lincoln and London, but after almost being apprehended at the Red Lion in Whitechapel, Dick Turpin is alleged to have fled northwards. According to legend, he changed his name to John Palmer and rode Black Bess on his epic journey into Yorkshire.

In order to sustain his lifestyle as a country gentleman, Turpin continued his criminal activities of horse stealing, sheep rustling and probably highway robbery, but it seems that boastful arrogance and threats against William Harris, landlord of the Ferry Inn at Brough, led to his demise.

Harris and others provided evidence to magistrates, who issued a warrant for Turpin's arrest. His false identity as 'John Palmer' was exposed and he was imprisoned in York Castle before being found guilty of horse stealing at a trial in March 1739. Such crimes carried the death penalty and his execution took place on 7 April 1739.

Access

St George's churchyard is located on George Street overlooking Piccadilly.

Dick Turpin's grave.

ROMAN REMAINS

FEATURES FROM THE HEYDAY OF EBORACUM

York has such an abundance of splendid old buildings that it is easy to overlook some of the fascinating Roman features.

Endless numbers of visitors pass through the abbey grounds but few probably give a second glance to the Multangular Tower. It is, in fact, a section of the Roman fortress that once covered the heart of the Roman settlement and was probably constructed on the orders of Emperor Constantine I during his term of office, between AD 308 and 337.

Closer examination of the upper level of the tower indicates that it was added during the thirteenth century, at a time when the medieval city wall was being completed.

Access

The Multangular Tower is within abbey grounds, close to the Museum Street entrance.
The Roman Column is set on the pavement on the south side of York Minster.
The Roman Bathhouse is in St Sampson's Square (close to the junction of Church Street and Silver Street).

Multangular Tower, abbey grounds.

Roman column, situated on the south side of York Minster.

A single tall column, set in the pavement on the south side of York Minster, was excavated from the south transept – where it had originally stood inside the great hall of the headquarters of the Roman Sixth Legion. Close inspection of the column shows that it is not, in fact, a single stone, but a series of slender bricks, which were later rendered.

The cellar area of the aptly-named 'Roman Bathhouse' in St Sampson's Square contains part of the frigidarium (cold room) and calidarium (hot room) of a fourth-century bathhouse. Each room has sections of the original walls and floor, with parts of the south-east and north-east walls of the frigidarium spreading 3ft wide and the same in height. A section of the cold plunge bath is also prominent, with tiles bearing the stamp of Legio VI and Legio IX.

Walls in the calidarium stand 4ft high and have a thickness of just over 5ft; heat was supplied from beneath the floor, which was supported on pilae (small brick piers) to a height of 2ft above the basement floor.

MARYGATE AND THE ABBEY WALLS

MONASTIC LINE OF DEFENCE

Access

Marygate runs between Bootham and the River Ouse.

Just about every corner of York holds historical interest and even a shor stretch of Marygate, between Bootham and the River Ouse, has several unusua features.

St Mary's Tower was originally constructed during the early fourteent century but it was badly damaged in the siege of 1644, when a mine was explode beneath the walls. Important records were lost in the ensuing blaze and fightin spilled into the abbey grounds before defenders held th line. Subsequent rebuilding of the tower was inexper and clumsy, making it easy to identify the original an later sections.

A considerable amount of defensive walling around S Mary's Abbey has survived – in fact more than any othe English monastic walls. Battlements along the uppe section of the defences provided a block of stonewor where archers could take cover before firing. A close view shows that wooden slats have been installed a shutters, to provide further protection after firing.

Abbey walls, Marygate.

YORK MINSTER

UNIQUE ECCLESIASTICAL TREASURES

York's crowning glory is undoubtedly the magnificent minster, which is arguably the most beautiful cathedral in the whole of Britain. The building has seen many phases of rebuilding and now stands upon the ruins of the Roman legionary fortress.

Early Saxon churches were replaced by a cruciform Norman minster and sizeable additions were made in the late twelfth century. The present building is the product of a succession of works completed between 1230 and 1470. Stone for building work was quarried from workings at Thevesdale, Bramham, Stapleton and Huddleston, and shipped by barge from Tadcaster, Wheldrake and Cawood to riverside wharves close to the minster.

Numbered among the minster's numerous treasures are 128 stained-glass windows dating from the twelfth century to present day. Many of these splendours are incorporated into the west front, where side towers reach almost 200ft skywards. Three styles of medieval building feature in this amazing frontage: the geometrical style of the fourteenth century at the lower level, the flowing style of the same century spreading across the centre, and impressive fifteenth-century work where the towers soar above the roof.

The Great East Window was completed in 1408 and contains the largest area of medieval stained glass in a single window, covering 194 square metres (which roughly equates to the size of a tennis court).

It depicts the beginning and end of the world, using scenes from the Book of Genesis and the Book of Revelation – the first and last books of the Bible. (The window was taken out of its frame in July 2008, as part of a £30 million restoration scheme, and

Access

York Minster faces High Petergate and Deangate on the north side of the city centre.

York Minster.

York Minster.

escaped unscathed at the end of December 2009 when fire broke out at the yar
in Minstergate where it was in storage.)

Within the minster, the Five Sisters Window has five lights over 50ft hig
and 5ft wide containing 1,250ft square of glass, made up of 100,000 pieces se
in lead brought from Rievaulx Abbey. The leafy design work was formed in
geometrical pattern and is said to be unrivalled in quality as well as quantity.

Widely regarded as the finest thirteenth-century window in existence,
contains a panel of the oldest glass in England. Dating from the Norman perioc
it is located at the base of the central light and portrays Daniel in the lions' den

four

Kingston-upon-Hull and Beverley

EASINGTON TITHE BARN

INTRIGUING REMINDER OF EARLIER CHURCH PRACTICES

Access

Easington is
18 miles east
of Hull via the
A1033 and
B1445.

All Saints' Church dominates the centre of the isolated village of Easington where rounded boulders from the beach add colour and character to this rural scene.

Set in a field on the south-west side of the church is a fine example of a tithe barn. Built of brick with a thatched roof, central porch and high wooden doors it is said to date from the fourteenth century and represents the only surviving example in East Yorkshire.

All Saints'
Church,
Easington.

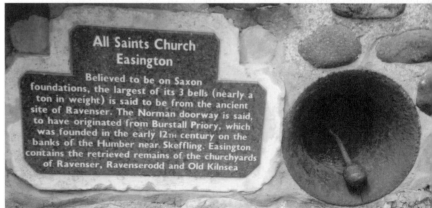

All Saints Church
Easington

Believed to be on Saxon foundations, the largest of its 3 bells (nearly a ton in weight) is said to be from the ancient site of Ravenser. The Norman doorway is said to have originated from Burstall Priory, which was founded in the early 12th century on the banks of the Humber near Skeffling. Easington contains the retrieved remains of the churchyards of Ravenser, Ravenserodd and Old Kilnsea

Tablet at
All Saints'
Church,
Easington.

ithe barn at Easington.

Tithes were first introduced in 794 in order to support parish priests or
monasteries and consisted of one tenth of the produce from the parish. This
could take the form of crops, livestock, dairy produce or profits from domestic
products.

In some areas, huge stone barns were built to store tithes and the practice
continued until 1936, when the Church of England ceased to collect tithes in
any form.

Some years ago the Easington tithe barn housed a collection of farm
implements and rural items, but at present it stands desolate and unused.

ELLOUGHTON – THE CASTLE

FANCIFUL DESIGNS IN AN URBAN SETTING

Access

Elloughton is
7 miles west
of Hull on the
south side of
the A63.

From a simple medieval ruin to grand Victorian edifices, the term 'castle' cover
a whole range of historic structures, and some certainly fit into the category c
'follies'.

'The Castle' at Elloughton, near Hull, dates from 1886 and overlooks the go
course at the end of Mill Lane. Surrounded by shrubs, its white-washed wall
include mock arrow loops below an array of decorative castellations.

'The Castle', Elloughton.

KILNSEA SOUND MIRROR

A LITTLE-KNOWN EARLY-WARNING DEFENCE SYSTEM

In recent years the early-warning defence systems at Fylingdales (south of Whitby) and Menwith Hill (near Harrogate) have made regular headlines, but these space-age installations represent only the latest attempt to defend England's eastern seaboard.

During the late fourth century AD, Roman forces constructed a line of signal stations along the Yorkshire coast and hill-top beacons gave warning of invasion during times of threat by the Spanish Armada and Napoleonic forces.

During the First World War, air raids by Zeppelins became a real danger and a series of concrete sound mirrors were positioned along the east coast in order to pick up sound waves from these enemy airships. Sounds were reflected off the concave 'mirror' surface into a trumpet mounted on a steel column and from there it was relayed to a stethoscope which allowed a 'listener' to determine the direction of an approaching aircraft.

Sound detection technology was replaced by 'reflective direction finding' – later known as radar – by the early 1940s, but these concrete acoustic mirrors continued in use until 1944.

Set in open country near the Beacon Lagoons Nature Reserve, this curious concrete structure measures 4m in height with 4m width and a base of 2m depth.

Access

From Kilnsea access is via a lane opposite the Blue Bell Information Centre, which runs alongside the caravan village to a point opposite the Beacon Lagoons Nature Reserve.

Kilnsea sound mirror.

CONSTABLE MAUSOLEUM, HALSHAM

STATELY, CIRCULAR, FINAL RESTING PLACE

Access

The Constable Mausoleum is on the north side of the B1362 to the north of Halsham village, 6 miles west of Withernsea.

Standing in splendid isolation, at the end of an avenue of yew trees in the villag of Halsham, is a fine, circular structure with domed stone roof and smooth pale-coloured walls. There is no indication about its use and a direct link wit this intriguing building – Halsham Hall, which stood on adjacent ground – ha long since been demolished.

It is, in fact, a mausoleum for the Constable family and was built for Edwar Constable of Burton Constable Hall between 1794 and 1802. He employe architect Thomas Atkinson to draw up designs, which included a fine doubl staircase leading up to the plinth on which the mausoleum is standing.

The nearby All Saints' Church has a number of memorials to the Constabl family. The mausoleum remains forlorn yet intact beside the B1362.

The Constable Mausoleum, Halsham.

CAVE CASTLE GATEHOUSE, SOUTH CAVE

UNLIKELY SENTINELS FOR THIS DAY AND AGE

Henry Hakewill specialised in building Tudor Gothic style castles and these included Cave Castle, which was completed in 1804. Alterations were made in 1875 and sections were demolished in the 1930s before it was adapted as an hotel.

It is believed that a medieval castle stood on the site some 800 years ago and the formidable gateposts beside the A1034 are more in keeping with the era of knights and fair maidens than with the main house or the gatehouse. Two bears guardant sit atop the gateways, which now lead to a housing estate.

Access

Cave Castle is on the north side of South Cave, 6 miles north of Brough via the A63.

Cave Castle gatehouse, South Cave.

Cave Castle gatepost.

THOMPSON'S FOLLY OR CASTLE HILL TOWER, COTTINGHAM

SOLITARY RELIC FROM A GRAND ESTATE

Access

Thompson's Folly is in the grounds of Castle Hill Hospital on the west side of Cottingham.

Surrounded by greenery in the grounds of Castle Hill Hospital at Cottingham, the Gothic style tower presents a forlorn prospect in this rather secluded setting. It was constructed in 1825 as a view point for the adjacent Cottingham Castle (built in 1816) and offered distant panoramas across the River Humber and 'the lovely land on every side', with a topograph to pinpoint landmarks. This was enriched further by appropriate texts from the writing of poets such as Goldsmith and Cowper.

Octagonal in shape, with pale cream brick walls and castellated parapet, the tower was part of the estate which belonged to the businessman and Member of Parliament, Thomas Thompson.

All other signs of the castle and estate have disappeared long ago to leave the tower as a skeletal reminder of earlier glories.

Castle Hill tower, Cottingham.

GREENWICH MERIDIAN

UNUSUAL ROADSIDE SIGNS

Roadside signs are usually few and far between in rural areas. Apart from the simple boards which give an indication of distances to nearby towns and villages, or warnings of impending bends and inclines, most verges merely display an array of all-year colour.

However, the information board and adjacent marble tablet close to the village of Patrington hold more than the usual amount of interest. Both mark the north-south Greenwich Meridian line that runs down the eastern side of England; the thin tablet of marble set in small pebbles was installed at this location in 2000.

Access

The Greenwich Meridian signs are ½ a mile south of Patrington beside the B1445 road.

Above & below: Greenwich Meridian.

HEDON – THE BOLINGBROKE CROSS

ROYAL LINKS WITH A RECOVERED RELIC

Access

Hedon is 5
miles east
of Hull via
the A1033
and B1362.
Holyrood
House is a
care home and
the privacy
of residents
should be
respected
when seeking
access through
an open
archway in
Magdalen
Lane.

During the medieval period Hedon flourished as a trading centre, with one natural and two man-made harbours, while three parish churches catered for the townspeople's spiritual needs. Shifting sands from the Humber estuary caused the port to silt up and trading outlets moved to the lost township of Ravenser (submerged some time ago in the North Sea), on Spurn Head and Hull.

Reminders of Hedon's earlier importance survive in the planned layout of the heart of the township, a fine church dedicated to St Augustine, and the civic mace. Engraved with the coats-of-arms of England and France, the mace was fashioned during the reign of Henry V (1413-22) and is believed to be the oldest in the country.

A rather different relic from the medieval period is to be found in the Garden of Holyrood House in Baxtergate. The Kilnsea Cross, or Bolingbroke Cross, was probably erected at Ravenser in 1399 to celebrate the landing of Henry Bolingbroke. Following the disappearance of this strip of coastline, it was washed

up at Kilnsea in 1818. From there it was moved to Hedon for safety and has a prominent position in the rear garden of Holyrood House. Standing to a height of 20ft, openwork around the top section is indistinct and figures around the shaft have not been clearly identified.

Bolingbroke Cross, Hedon.

NORTH BAR, BEVERLEY

AN ENTRY POINT OF IRREGULAR, MEDIEVAL BRICKWORK

The North Bar makes a highly appropriate entrance to the attractive locations around Beverley's town centre. Completed in 1409, it is made up of a total of 125,000 bricks of varying sizes. Few measure more than 2in in thickness but often they have a length of nearly 10in, as early brick-makers were unable to maintain consistent temperature in their kilns. The discrepancy in brick sizes was overcome by varying the amount of mortar applied around them.

Closer inspection of this fine brick structure indicates a vaulted archway – with posterns on either side – and stepped battlements along the upper level.

Access

North Bar is at the junction of the A1035 York Road and A164 Driffield Road on the north-west side of Beverley.

North Bar, Beverley.

BEVERLEY MINSTER

A FINE CHURCH WITH OUTSTANDING FEATURES

Towards the end of the seventh century, John of Beverley constructed an early church and monastery on the site of Beverley Minster. The present church is the fourth building on the site. It is larger than some cathedrals and has the rare shape of a double cross (Lorraine Cross), which illustrates the strong French influence. Another indication of this connection is the dedication – the parish church of St John and St Martin (patron saint of France).

Building work covers three main phases, beginning with Early English work (1220-60) behind the high altar at the east end and continuing in the Decorated style (1308-49) and Perpendicular work (1380-1420) at the west end.

Access

Beverley Minster is at the southern end of the town between Minster Moorgate on the south side and Lord Roberts Road on the north side.

Beverley Minster.

Several of the church's finest features are located at the east end of the building and these include the Percy Shrine and adjacent Frid Stool. The simple tomb is believed to have been built as the final resting place of Eleanor FitzAlan, wife of the First Lord Percy; in contrast to the tomb, the richly-decorated canopy is often cited as a masterpiece of the decorated Gothic style. The Frid Stool, a simple stone chair, was endowed as a sanctuary seat in AD 937 by King Athelstan, and this meant that the Peace of St John of Beverley extended in every direction for a mile round the church. For centuries, fugitives from justice who sat in the Frid Stool had thirty days' grace whilst Church officials tried to make peace between fugitive and accuser. If no agreement could be reached then the criminal was escorted from the minster. The right of sanctuary was curtailed in 1548 and ended in the early seventeenth century.

The chancel is the setting for an amazing collection of choir stalls. Carved in the early sixteenth century by craftsmen from Ripon, each misericord (or mercy seat) has a different carving on the underside and these include an ape on a horse, a woman beating her husband while the dog steals from a cauldron, and a woman being led to a ducking stool. They represent the largest collection of misericords in their original condition anywhere in the country.

Beverley Minster clock is unique as it is the only church clock which chimes in two towers. It was crafted by Smith & Co. of Derby and chimed for the first time on 15 February 1902. As well as striking each quarter hour on ten bells in the north tower, it also sounds the hours on the large 7 tonne bell, known as 'Big John', in the south tower.

High above the central section of the minster, set in the roof space, is a tread wheel which would originally have been used to lift building materials to upper levels. It was installed during a programme of work carried out by Nicholas Hawksmoor between 1716 and 1737 and is claimed to be the only tread wheel still in working order in a church.

ST MARY'S CHURCH, BEVERLEY

CELEBRATED CARVINGS IN ONE OF THIS COUNTRY'S FINEST PARISH CHURCHES

Access

St Mary's Church is located at the junction of Hengate and North Bar Within.

Occupying a central position in the township and with a range of splendid architectural details, St Mary's Church is frequently mistaken for the minster itself. Indeed it is often hailed, with some justification, as one of the most beautiful parish churches in the whole country.

Building work began in the twelfth century but most of the present structure dates from the fourteenth and fifteenth centuries. The light-coloured stonework of the walls measures nearly 200ft from east to west and includes a massive tower soaring 99ft high to a crownpiece with sixteen pinnacles. During a service in 1520 the tower collapsed into the nave roof causing fatal injuries to several worshippers, and in 1604 the south aisle gave way after it was struck by a bolt of lightening. The whole church was restored during the nineteenth century by A.W.N. Pugin and Sir Gilbert Scott.

The imposing south porch has a wealth of buttresses, niches and slender pinnacles. This arrangement continues within the spacious interior where heads of medieval folk decorate the arcading and, on the north side, angels hold shields showing the names of those who gave the arches and pillars. (These include the Good Wives of Beverley and, best known of all, the Beverley Minstrels.)

A doorway in the north choir aisle leads to a crypt under a raised chapel with a fine roof which has bosses showing the Four Evangelists, a bear eating grapes, a man on horseback, a man fighting a dragon and a fox preaching to geese. Corbels under the roof have carvings of a man playing bagpipes, a fiddler, men with a flute and a harp, and lion heads.

Perhaps most curious of all is an arched doorway in the main aisle. It is guarded by a lion and a well-dressed hare holding a staff and carrying a satchel over its shoulder; the claim is often made that this fine carving was the inspiration for the March Hare in *Alice's Adventures in Wonderland*.

Writing under the pen name Lewis Carroll, Charles Lutwidge Dodgson (1832-98) was a frequent visitor to Beverley and it is distinctly possible that the array of strange creatures in St Mary's Church and the nearby minster were responsible for firing his imagination.

St Mary's
Church,
Beverley.

WHITE HORSE INN, BEVERLEY

MEMORIES OF AN EARLIER LADY LICENSEE AT 'NELLIE'S'

As one of Beverley's oldest hostelries, the White Horse Inn has a great deal of atmosphere. There is no indication about its origins as an inn, but brickwork now covers the timber-framed late medieval style (which originally included a projecting first floor).

There is documentary evidence that the site of the present public house belonged to Church authorities from 1585 and the first reference to an inn is dated 1666. A range of outbuildings, including stables, have been used through the years, but the present set of rooms at the rear of the inn was added in the 1830s. Brickwork dates from the late seventeenth or early eighteenth century and the White Horse Inn's walls once had a lime-wash covering of yellow ochre. Along with dark red shutters, this pale wall covering reflected the colours of the Sykes family from Sledmere, who represented the town in Parliament.

The White Horse Inn's rooms have accommodated a wide range of patrons, including travellers, farmers, landowners, visitors to the Norwood Cattle Market, and visitors to the annual Martinmas Fair – which was held in early November.

Access

The White Horse Inn is situated on Hengate between North Bar Within and New Walkergate.

In 1927 St Mary's Church sold the inn to Francis Collinson; after his death it was run by his eldest son, William, and then Francis' daughter Nellie. During her time as licensee, the White Horse Inn became affectionately known as 'Nellie's'.

In 1976 the Samuel Smith Brewery, based at Tadcaster, took over ownership and since then essential modernisation has been carried out in areas such as toilet and kitchen facilities. Public rooms, however, have retained features such as open fires and stone-flagged floors that give the White Horse Inn such a distinctive and intriguing atmosphere.

The White Horse Inn, Beverley.

WHITE TELEPHONE BOXES, BEVERLEY

A PALER SHADE OF CALLING SERVICE

Access

White telephone boxes are to be found at town centre locations around Beverley.

With the growing popularity of mobile phones, old-style telephone boxes are few and far between. Traditional red-painted telephone boxes attract a measure of interest but white telephone boxes are even more of a rarity.

In fact, the white telephone boxes of Hull's telephone system are unique and their presence on Beverley's Georgian streets adds interest and style to the elegant setting. Hull City Council opened its first exchange in 1904 and for many years it remained the only municipal telephone company in the country.

It never became part of the national telephone service and since privatisation it has retained unique status as the only publicly-owned service in the country.

White telephone boxes, Beverley.

SKIDBY MILL

EAST YORKSHIRE'S ONLY WORKING WINDMILL

Sitting proudly on high ground between Hessle and Beverley, Skidby Mill is said to be the only windmill in working order in East Yorkshire. Its tall, narrow tower, cap, and sails, date in part from 1821, with an extension completing the current five storeys in 1870.

A recent inspection by engineers from East Riding Council highlighted the need to replace a number of structural timbers, as well as the four sails, and work was carried out in 2009. The first flour from the renovated mill was produced, with due ceremony, at the end of June 2009.

Skidby Mill has become a highly popular tourist attraction and it also houses the Museum of East Riding Rural Life.

Access

Skidby Mill occupies a prominent position on the west side of the A164 between Hessle and Beverley.

Skidby Mill.

Skidby Mill information board.

Farm items at Skidby Mill.

PRINCES QUAY SHOPPING CENTRE, HULL

RETAIL OUTLETS THAT SEEM TO FLOAT ON WATER

Access

The Princes Quay Shopping Centre is north of Hull Marina with access from Princes Dock Street.

Princes Dock, originally known as Junction Dock, was constructed between 1826 and 1829 close to Kingston-upon-Hull Old Town area; for many years it was at the hub of commercial activity on the waterfront.

Recent regeneration schemes have transformed large areas of downtown Hull and in June 1984 the city council invited proposals to develop vacant sites and improve the dockland area. Four years later work got underway on the Princes Dock area at a cost of £65,000,000 and developers have attempted to continue the original nautical theme of the city.

Rather than fill in the dock, the Princes Quay complex was constructed on more than 500 stilts so that it appears to float above the water. The maritime theme is continued through balustrade porthole light fittings, patterns in floor tiles, signs and compass rose logo.

The whole shopping centre houses more than eighty retail units and opened to the general public on 15 March 1991.

The Princes Quay Shopping Centre, Hull.

HULL TOWN WALLS

DRAMATIC EPISODES IN THE TOWN'S HISTORY

The earliest form of settlement at Hull was a small medieval township named Wyke. Inhabitants were mainly involved in fishing and this area of land was under the ownership of monks from the Cistercian abbey of Meaux, near Beverley.

During 1293 King Edward I purchased the village of Wyke from the abbot of Meaux and began to develop the site's potential as a harbour and military base. The growing township was named Kingston-upon-Hull because it was situated on the River Hull and belonged to the king.

Access

The exposed sections of the city walls and site of Beverley Gate are at the western end of Whitefriargate.

Beverley Gate plaque.

Medieval Hull, now known as the Old Town, developed close to the west bank of the River Hull and the town's first charter was granted in 1299. As its importance grew Hull gained a mint and a ferry link to Lincolnshire, and there was a period of prosperity under the de la Pole family. William de la Pole became Hull's first mayor and received a knighthood from the king. The de la Poles received trading privileges and government offices in return for loaning cash to fund overseas campaigns, and Hull was often involved in national events and royal visits.

In 1537 the township was drawn into the Pilgrimage of Grace and four years later Henry VIII made a visit to Catherine Howard. The king is said to have been so impressed by his reception that he handed over his own sword as a gift to the community. Puritan followers are believed to have visited Hull in search of a Dutch captain to transport them to Holland – years before they sailed in the *Mayflower* to America. After their arrival in the New World, a town near Boston Harbour was named Hull.

Events on 23 April 1642 formed one of the most dramatic episodes in Hull history. King Charles I rode from Beverley to Hull, with around 300 troops only to be refused entry by the governor, Sir John Hotham. This action is said to represent the first overt act of the Civil War.

Subsequent growth saw Hull become not only the country's leading fishing port but also a major centre for the seed-crushing and oil-extricating industry. The milling industry and timber imports from the Baltic region featured in the many miles of quays and warehouses that spread along the river frontage.

Much of this early heritage was lost during wartime bombing raids and recent phases of re-development; there are still clues to these aspects of Hull's history not only through unusual street names such as Dagger Lane, Bowlalley Lane, Fish Street and Sewer Street but also in an exposed area of the town walls.

A plaque highlights the location of Beverley Gate where Sir John Hotham famously defied King Charles I on 23 April 1642 and initiated events of the Civil War.

THE WILBERFORCE MONUMENT

GRAND MEMORIAL TO A LOCAL HUMANITARIAN CAMPAIGNER

The large sunken garden area known as Queen's Gardens covers the former Queen's Dock, which was constructed during 1775-8. At the eastern end, the view is dominated by an enormous column in commemoration of William Wilberforce.

Standing 90ft high, the Doric-style column stands on a large Grecian base decorated with wreaths and urns. Born in Hull in 1759, he studied at the town's grammar school before graduating from Cambridge University. It was here that he developed a keen interest in politics and from 1785 this was allied with an involvement with moral causes and social reform.

A strong Christian faith sustained Wilberforce's campaign to abolish slavery, with support from individuals such as William Pitt and Thomas Clarkson. While on his deathbed, 26 July 1833, Wilberforce heard news that the House of Commons had passed a Bill to abolish the slave trade throughout the British Empire. The monument carries the simple statement – 'Negro Slavery Abolished 1 August MDCCCXXXIV'.

Wilberforce House, on the High Street, was the birthplace of William Wilberforce and houses a display relating to the slave trade and the campaign to abolish slavery.

Access

The Wilberforce monument dominates the east end of Queen's Gardens beside Wilberforce Drive. Wilberforce House is located at the northern end of the High Street close to Drypool Bridge.

The Wilberforce monument.

Inscription on the Wilberforce monument.

HOLY TRINITY CHURCH, HULL

THE COUNTRY'S LARGEST PARISH CHURCH

Access

Holy Trinity Church is located between North Church Side and South Church Side with Market Place to the east and the Open Market to the west.

In terms of area covered, Holy Trinity Church is claimed to be the largest parish church in England. Cruciform in shape, it measures 285ft from east to west and almost 100ft along the transept, while the massive central tower rises 150ft.

Building phases range from early fourteenth-century work in the transepts, mid-fourteenth century in the chancel, and a period spanning the end of the fourteenth and beginning of the fifteenth centuries for the nave. The tower was added in the years around AD 1500. The transepts and lower levels of the crossing tower are brick, representing the earliest significant use of brickwork in this country.

Surprisingly, Holy Trinity served only as a chapel of ease until 1661, when it officially became a parish church, and it remained intact during heavy wartime bombing raids.

The lofty interior has a fine array of windows, soaring arcades and narrow pillars with fine screens, and at a lower level the impressive stone pulpit is reached by a spreading staircase. The brass eagle lectern was presented to mark John Bromby's fifty years of ministry as vicar at Holy Trinity, which began in 1797. In fact, he continued for another twenty years to complete one of the longest periods of service in the country.

A curious story surrounds the painting of 'The Last Supper' by James Parmentier. Completed in 1711, it was presented to the church at Hessle but was too large to pass through the door. A disciple at one end of the painting was cut away but it was still too large and, even after another figure had been removed, the picture still would not pass through Hessle church doorway. The solution was to display it at Holy Trinity – with only ten of the twelve disciples remaining.

Left: Holy Trinity Church, Hull.

Right: Plaque at Holy Trinity Church.

HUMBER FERRY BOOKING OFFICE

ISSUING TICKETS BUT NO SIGN OF A TRAIN

Occupying a fine riverfront position, the former Humber Ferry booking office dates from 1880 and is often described as the only railway station in England never to have seen a train. In order to take a train journey, it was necessary to cross the river by paddle steamer from Victoria Pier to New Holland.

The ferry service closed during 1981 when the Humber Bridge was opened (bringing to an end ferry operations, which were first recorded in 1315).

Access

The former Humber Ferry booking office is on Nelson Street on the east side of Hull Marina.

Humber Ferry plaque.

Humber Ferry booking office.

SPURN LIGHTSHIP

FLASHING A WARNING TO SEA-GOING VESSELS

Spurn Lightship spent fifty years of service as a navigational aid at a location 4½ miles east of Spurn Point. Measuring 33m in length, this steel plate double-hull tower lightship has now found a calmer mooring in Hull Marina.

After a programme of restoration by Hull City Council, it is open during the summer months for visitors to inspect the master's cabin, crew's quarters, galley and lifeboat.

Access

Spurn Lightship is moored in Hull Marina. Open on Mondays – Saturdays 10 a.m. – 5 p.m. and Sunday 1.30 p.m. – 4.30 p.m. April to October. Small admission charge.

Spurn Lightship.

THE DEEP

A BOLD SYMBOL OF HULL'S REGENERATION

Access

The Deep is at the confluence of the River Hull and the Humber estuary to the south of Garrison Road.

The dramatic outlines of the world's only submarium dominate the river frontage at Sammy's Point – an area at the confluence of the River Hull and the Humber estuary that is named after Martin Samuelson, a nineteenth-century industrialist and civic leader.

'The Deep' took three years to construct at a cost of £45.5 million and involved twenty-nine separate works contract packages. A structure of this size, with so many innovative design features, inevitably provides a host of impressive statistics, including: the deepest aquarium tank in Europe at 10m; the deepest underwater acrylic tunnel in Europe; a 'skimmer tower' for purifying water, which is the largest in the world with a capacity of 1,500 cubic metres an hour.

Its primary role is as a visitor attraction, and members of the public follow a route that runs gently downhill through the building then upwards to the starting point. The overall theme of the exhibition is that it transports the visitor from the 'dawn of time' – as illustrated by the 'Big Bang' origin of the universe – through oceans of past, present and future. Along the way there are no less than 2,800 marine creatures living in the huge tanks.

Yet this amazing structure has much more to offer. It includes a business centre and also The Deep Research Facility, which is run by the University of Hull and includes the largest 'total environment simulator' in Europe to re-create estuarial tidal flow and sediments. Viewing platforms, at a height of 24m above sea level, make excellent vantage points for the city. Above all, 'The Deep' has the role of a regeneration pioneer in this area of Hull, forging a link between the old city and the previously isolated large, new housing development to the east on the former Victoria Dock.

The Deep.

HUMBER BRIDGE

A MAJOR FEAT OF CIVIL ENGINEERING

Access

The A15 leads to the Humber Bridge on the west side of Hessle (north bank) and Barton upon Humber (south bank).

For over a century, campaigners argued for the construction of a bridge o[r] tunnel across the Humber before work on the hugely impressive suspensio[n] bridge got underway in 1973. As early as 1872 proposals were put forward fo[r] a tunnel scheme, and the Depression years of the late 1920s and early 1930[s] ended plans for a multi-span truss bridge that were formulated in 1928. Difficul[t] geological formations ended plans for a tunnel – on grounds of expense – an[d] shifting channels ruled out a more traditional bridge with mid-river support[s]. But, in 1959, approval was given for a suspension bridge.

A ferry service across the Humber existed in Roman times betwee[n] Winteringham and Brough and, until the opening of the bridge on 17 July 198[1] travellers had the choice of a twenty-minute ferry crossing or a road journe[y] which covered 48 more miles (between Hull and Grimsby) than the bridg[e] crossing. Before the bridge was completed, around 90,000 vehicles used th[e] ferry each year and by 2007 some 120,000 vehicles were crossing the bridge eac[h] week.

Following its official opening by HM The Queen, the Humber Bridg[e] remained the world's longest single-span suspension bridge for seventeen year[s] before larger structures were constructed in Denmark, Japan and China, but i[t] remains the world's longest bridge that ca[n] be crossed on foot.

This amazing structure has becom[e] a tourist attraction in its own right an[d] its appeal is increased by the 48-acr[e] Humber Bridge Country Park whic[h] opened in 1986 on the site of an ancien[t] chalk quarry. A lengthy list of statistic[s] includes the facts that 480,000 tonnes o[f] concrete, 27,500 tonnes of steel and 8[0] acres of painted steelwork are include[d] in its superstructure. The whole bridge i[s] constantly in motion and it bends mor[e] than 10ft during winds of 80mph, with th[e] towers swaying inwards at the top.

The estimated lifespan for the Humbe[r] Bridge is 120 years.

Humber Bridge.

WITHERNSEA LIGHTHOUSE

AN INLAND GUIDING LIGHT FOR SEA-GOING MEN

On 20 October 1890, a Grimsby-based fishing vessel, *Genesta*, smashed into Withernsea pier and the ship's captain was lost overboard. At the inquest into his death, the coroner expressed doubts that the tragedy would have happened if a shore-based warning light had been operating at Withernsea.

Access

The lighthouse is on the south side of the B1362 Hull Road.

Following the results of the inquest, construction of a lighthouse got underway in 1891 and on 1 March 1894 the first beam flashed out over the North Sea. Built of brick and concrete, its snow-white walls measure 127ft in height and have a depth of 5ft. Foundations are 15ft below ground to support the octagonal walls which represent an unusual architectural design.

Unlike most lighthouses, it does not stand on a coastline position but is to be found some distance inland, among houses on the busy B1362. A spiral staircase, with 144 steps around interior walls, leads to the light room and viewing platform. The structure is topped by a wind vane in the shape of a 6ft-long golden arrow, which is connected to a compass in the light room.

After some eighty-two years of operational service, apart from blackouts during the two world wars, the lighthouse flashed its last beam in 1976. Originally the two lighthouse keepers lived in the adjoining house and cottage, and the overall number of shipwrecks was reduced. Withernsea lifeboat *Docea Chapman* was withdrawn from service in 1913 by the RNLI, but during 1974 the local lifeboat station was reopened.

Following closure of the lighthouse, it was adapted to accommodate a museum of local history items and Royal National Lifeboat Institute materials.

Withernsea lighthouse.

WITHERNSEA PIER

SHADES OF A MEDIEVAL CASTLE – ON THE SEA FRONT

Access

Withernsea is
15 miles east
of Hull via the
B1362.

The growth of seaside resorts during the mid-nineteenth century led to th
construction of piers as an added attraction for holiday-makers; between 186
and 1910 roughly ninety seaside pleasure piers were completed around th
coastline of Great Britain and the Isle of Man.

A pier was opened at the newly-established resort of Saltburn in 1869 an
others followed on the Yorkshire coast at Scarborough (1869), Redcar (1873
Coatham (1875), Withernsea (1878) and Hornsea (1880), but by 1910 four c
them had already been demolished.

Saltburn pier narrowly escaped demolition in 1974 and now claims th
distinction of being Yorkshire's only surviving seaside pleasure pier. There ar
few tangible reminders of other piers, but Withernsea has an intriguing featur
from the heyday of its pier.

Withernsea pier was completed in 1878 at a cost of £12,000 and patrons coul
pay a penny to stroll along the 1,196ft-long structure. Seating ran the full lengt
and a saloon provided refreshments.

Withernsea pier.

The entrance to the pier was dominated by a large castelled gateway omplete with turrets and towers. It soon earned the nickname 'The Sandcastle' nd initially drew large numbers of day visitors from the nearby city of Hull. ut, on 28 October 1880, a ferocious storm battered the Yorkshire coast.

Both Redcar and Hornsea piers were badly damaged by ship collisions and Vithernsea pier was struck by two vessels, the *Jabez* and *Saffron*. Repairs were arried out, but on 28 March 1882 a raging storm swept away the pier head and aloon.

Further damage followed during the night of 20 October 1890 when Grimsby shing boat *Genesta* collided with it during more foul weather; Withernsea pier's ate was sealed on 22 March 1893 when the *Henry Parr* smashed into it. A short ection of about 50ft survived until 1903, when it was removed during work on he sea wall and promenade.

The castellated entrance was left in place and over the years it has served a umber of functions. During the Edwardian period the north tower housed the Beach Master's office, while the south tower became a penny bazaar and gift hop. The whole area proved to be ideal for staging pierrot shows.

In the 1950s the south tower was adapted as a coastguard station, and this anciful structure – known affectionately as the 'Pier Towers', 'Pier Head' or The Castle' – continues to be popular as an instantly recognisable meeting oint.

SPURN PENINSULA / POINT

FRAGILE BARRIER AGAINST NORTH SEA BREAKERS

The 3½ mile-long finger of land that extends from the Yorkshire mainland lmost to the middle of the Humber estuary represents one of the most mportant sand and shingle spits in the country.

Spurn Peninsula is formed from sand and shingle swept from the eroding cliffs of the Holderness area and then deposited to form a long embankment in heltered waters within the mouth of the Humber estuary. Winds remove sand rom the beaches and heap it into dunes and the growth of marram grass traps more sand. Waves move sand and pebbles along the beach on the seaward side of Spurn to its furthest point, with the effect that the peninsula continues to grow n length.

Study of old maps and documents indicates that the spit of land forming Spurn Point has an average 260-year cycle as it shifts along an east-west axis with the inevitable loss of towns and villages. Most notable of these was probably Ravenser, which was a town of some importance during the early fourteenth

Access

Spurn Point runs south from Kilnsea, on the most easterly point of the coast, via the A1033 to Patrington (from Hull) and B1445 to Easington.

126

Spurn
Peninsula.

century with a weekly market and annual fair. However, by 1346 about two thirds of the town had already disappeared below North Sea waves and destruction was complete by around 1360.

Even before the medieval period there were references to Spurn or to earlier spits; in about AD 670, a monk named Wilgils set up a small monastery on what was described as a promontory surrounded by the sea, and in about 950 the hero of the Icelandic narrative, *Egil's Saga*, was wrecked near the seaward point.

The first reference to Spurn Head on a map was in 1564, before it was breached and swept away by the sea in about 1608. Subsequent regeneration of the spit saw construction of a lighthouse by Justiman Angell in 1673-4 and in the following year it was being called Spurn Point.

Angell's lighthouse was swept away just as the eminent engineer John Smeaton was completing new lighthouses in 1772-6. During the Napoleonic Wars barracks and gun batteries were constructed. The fear of invasion by French forces passed and in 1810 the first lifeboat station was set up in the redundant barracks.

During the mid-nineteenth century, erosion took a greater toll on Spurn Point and in December 1849 a north-westerly storm caused a breach measuring over ¼ mile across the spit. Further breaches in 1851 and 1856 left Spurn as a series of islands at high water; the government approved repairs to the breach and the positioning of groynes along the shoreline during the 1860s.

Bull Fort was built at Spurn in the First World War and was connected to un batteries at Kilnsea by railway. The rail link was used by steam locomotives, vehicle with a petrol engine and a truck with a sail. Military buildings were lded in the Second World War and the railway was replaced by a road. Huge oncrete blocks, that were meant to prevent an enemy landing in wartime, have een repositioned at a location now known as Narrow Neck where the North ea is most likely to break through the narrow neck of land.

Any future breach of Spurn would have a serious impact on the rest of the Iumber estuary and the Environment Agency has drawn up a plan for protecting ie estuary from flooding – which includes repairing any breach in Spurn Head.

Spurn Point is also the base for lifeboat men and their families. Seven homes ccommodate the only full-time crew in the country, with their lifeboat moored : the end of a nearby jetty. Associated British Ports also operates pilots from ere to control the safe passage of Humber cargo vessels, which currently nounts to 30 per cent of all the UK's shipped tonnage.

In 1960 the Yorkshire Naturalists Trust became owners of the Spurn Peninsula id the rich variety of animal, plant and bird life led to its designation as a nature eserve, which covers 280 acres of land above high watermark as well as around 77 acres of foreshore between high and low watermarks.

BIBLIOGRAPHY

BOOKS

Easdown, Martin, *Piers of Disaster: The Sad Story of the Seaside Pleasure Piers of th*
  Yorkshire Coast (Hutton Press; 1996)
Headley, Gwyn & Meulenkamp, Wim, *Follies, Grottoes and Garden Building*
  (Autumn Press Ltd; 1999)
Mee, Arthur, *The King's England: Yorkshire East Riding and City of Yor*
  (Hodder & Stoughton; 1942)
Muir, Richard, *Old Yorkshire* (Michael Joseph Ltd; 1987)
Pevsner, Nikolaus, *Yorkshire: York and the East Riding* (Penguin Books Ltd; 2001
Rennison, Eileen, *In Search of the Unusual in East Yorkshire and the Yorkshire Coas*
  (Hutton Press; 1997)
Ryder, Peter F., *Medieval Buildings of Yorkshire* (Moorland Publishing Co. Ltd; 1982

LOCAL GUIDES AND MONOGRAPHS

Flamborough, St Oswald's Church
Kingston-upon-Hull, Holy Trinity Parish Church
Market Weighton Civic Society, Giant Bradley Heritage Trail
Market Weighton, History of All Saints' Church
Pocklington Town Guide
York Minster, Canon Reginald Grant

ARTICLES

Variously published in issues of *Yorkshire Life* magazine, *Yorkshire Riding*
magazine and *Darlington and Stockton Times*, *Northern Echo* and *Yorkshire Po*
newspapers.

MISCELLANEOUS GUIDES AND PAMPHLETS

Beverley's Historical Buildings
Humber Bridge – Visitors' Guide
Spurn Peninsula Nature Reserve
White Horse Inn – A Brief History of Nellie's
York Unitarians – Saint Saviourgate Unitarian Chapel